Introduction to BASIC

Introduction to BASIC
A case study approach

P. J. Hartley
Senior Lecturer in Numerical Mathematics
Lanchester Polytechnic, Coventry

M

© P. J. Hartley 1976

All rights reserved. No part of this publication may be reproduced or transmitted, in any form or by any means, without permission

First published 1976 by
THE MACMILLAN PRESS LTD
London and Basingstoke
Associated companies in New York Dublin
Melbourne Johannesburg and Madras

ISBN 0 333 19620 1

Printed and bound in Great Britain
by Unwin Brothers Limited,
The Gresham Press, Old Woking, Surrey

This book is sold subject to the standard conditions of the Net Book Agreement.

The paperback edition of this book is sold subject to the condition that it shall not, by way of trade or otherwise, be lent, re-sold, hired out, or otherwise circulated without the publisher's prior consent in any form of binding or cover other than that in which it is published and without a similar condition including this condition being imposed on the subsequent purchaser.

CONTENTS

	Preface	vii
1	Introduction	1
	1.1 Who for and what for	
	1.2 Contents and format	
2	The Computer System and You	3
	2.1 Introduction	
	2.2 The computer system	
	2.3 Modes of operation	
3	Problem-solving	7
	3.1 Who does what	
	3.2 Algorithms	
	3.3 Flow charts	
	3.4 Case study - linear interpolation	
	3.5 An improved linear interpolation algorithm	
	3.6 Trace tables	
	3.7 A further improved linear interpolation algorithm	
	3.8 Postscript	
	Exercises	
4	BASIC - The First Essentials	21
	4.1 Case study - linear interpolation Mark 1	
	4.2 BASIC requirements	
	4.3 A program for the case study	
	4.4 Check your progress	
	4.5 A second case study - the area of a triangle	
	4.6 Strings	
	4.7 A program for the area of a triangle	
	Exercises	
5	BASIC - Loops and Branches	34
	5.1 Case study - linear interpolation Mark 2	
	5.2 BASIC requirements	
	5.3 A program for the case study	
	5.4 Check your progress	
	5.5 A second case study - graph-plotting on a terminal	
	5.6 Output formats	
	5.7 Standard functions	
	5.8 A program for the graph-plotting case study	
	5.9 Postscript	
	Exercises	

6	Programming Practice		48

    6.1   Introduction
    6.2   Typical mistakes
    6.3   Editing programs
    6.4   Program-testing
    6.5   Documentation
    Exercises

7	BASIC - Arrays		55

    7.1   Case study - linear interpolation Mark 3
    7.2   One-dimensional arrays in BASIC
    7.3   FOR loops
    7.4   Check your progress
    7.5   A program for the case study
    7.6   A second case study - matrix manipulation
    7.7   Two-dimensional arrays in BASIC
    7.8   Check your progress
    7.9   A program for the matrix manipulation problem
    7.10 Postscript
    Exercises

8	BASIC- Functions		72

    8.1   Case study - numerical integration
    8.2   User-defined functions in BASIC
    8.3   Check your progress
    8.4   A program for the case study
    8.5   A second case study - solving an equation
    8.6   A program for Newton's method
    Exercises

9	BASIC - Subroutines		85

    9.1   Case study - more numerical integration
    9.2   Subroutines in BASIC
    9.3   A program for the case study
    9.4   Check your progress
    9.5   A second case study - a queueing problem
    9.6   A program for the queueing problem
    Exercises

10	BASIC - Matrix Operations		96

    10.1 Introduction
    10.2 Matrix algebra - a brief summary
    10.3 Matrix statements I
    10.4 Case study - an electrical network problem
    10.5 Matrix statements II
    10.6 A program for the case study
    10.7 A second case study - a vibration problem
    10.8 Matrix statements III
    10.9 A program for the inverse power method
    10.10 Postscript - redimensioning
    Exercises

References and further reading   115

Solutions to selected exercises   116

PREFACE

Many scientists and technologists working today in the areas of design, research and development have access to a digital computer system. To use such a system to help them solve their problems they need two skills: the ability to converse with the computer and the ability to apply, adapt and invent numerical methods of solution. This book is concerned primarily with the first of these skills, but is inevitably involved with the second as well.

Conversing with a computer means being able to write computer programs in a computer language. This book introduces the computer language BASIC (Beginners' All-purpose Symbolic Instruction Code), which was originally developed in the 1960s in the United States as a simple, 'conversational', computer language for college students. Since then BASIC has been further developed to a stage where it is widely used outside the purely educational field. It is considered by many practitioners to be the best available compromise between the simplicity required to make a computer language usable by non-professionals and the sophistication required to realise the power of a modern computer system.

Computer-programming courses and books vary in their aims from those for computer scientists at one extreme to the gentlest of appreciation courses at the other. Here I have tried to give a working introduction to BASIC programming for undergraduate and H.N.D. students of science and engineering. I believe that the text is sufficiently complete for those who are to use a computer as part of their other studies, also that it will be suitable as an introduction to computing for those who are not. It will also serve as a useful introduction to the subject for practising scientists and technologists.

The book is unusual in two respects. Firstly, it does not attempt to be comprehensive: the details that I have found to be important to students are included, but I have deliberately set out to avoid the appearance and pedantry of a BASIC manual. If the reader requires more detail than appears here then he can, and perhaps should, consult the relevant manual for the computer in question. Secondly, I have sought to reverse the usual order, which introduces BASIC statements and commands and then gives examples of their use (often trivial, and often not showing why the statement or command is really needed). To this end all the chapters on BASIC have one or two case studies that are used to introduce and show the need for the elements of the language. The computer system is thus shown as a problem-solving tool rather than a super-toy.

Although the solution of these case-study problems often involves some use of numerical mathematics, the techniques are usually simple (linear interpolation and the trapezium rule, for example). In each case I have described the numerical method briefly, and given a reference to a suitable book for more details and further reading.

All but the first two chapters have exercises appended to them, and some selected solutions are given at the end of the book. In most cases where a new element of BASIC is introduced there is a 'check your progress' section designed to test comprehension of the material.

I believe that the book would be used to most advantage in a course of some twenty to twenty-five hours duration. It could be made suitable for a fifteen-hour course by omitting chapters 8,9 and 10, and for an even shorter course by omitting chapter 7 as well. Considerable gain would accrue to the students if they had access to computer terminals - because the book is biased towards the interactive use of BASIC - but they are not a prerequisite facility.

That this book exists is in great part due to my mother, Gwyneth Hartley, who typed the text quickly and accurately, and to the staff of the Macmillan Press who asked me to write it in the first place and who were so helpful through all stages of its production. My grateful thanks also go to Lanchester Polytechnic for allowing me to use their computer facilities for the testing of the programs in the book. The figures that show output from a computer terminal were produced on their ICL 1903S system. Lastly, the credit for the flow-chart outlines and other diagrams goes to Ken Waller, also of Lanchester Polytechnic.

P.J. Hartley

1 INTRODUCTION

1.1 WHO FOR AND WHAT FOR

The primary aim of this book is to teach students of the sciences (including engineering) how to use an electronic digital computer to calculate solutions to problems. All of the examples used in the book involve real problems, however simple, but they have been chosen to illustrate the text and not to provide ready-made computer packages for the solution of general classes of problem.

The book is designed for undergraduate and H.N.D. students of engineering and science, but it is equally suitable for any student at that level, provided that he is willing to accept the scientific bias of the examples and has the mathematical maturity to understand the methods of solution employed.

1.2 CONTENTS AND FORMAT

The first six chapters of the book provide the elementary knowledge required to write and run computer programs using the computer language BASIC. The examples used in these chapters are correspondingly simple so that the subject matter is not obscured by the problems used to illustrate it.

Chapters 7 to 10 contain details of the more powerful aspects of BASIC, but only chapter 10 requires mathematical concepts (those of matrix algebra) that might be outside the experience of the readers for whom the book is intended.

One of the difficulties facing any author of a book on BASIC is that its implementation varies from computer to computer. The elements of the language that are presented in this book are common to most computer systems, although many of them will have BASIC facilities additional to the ones described here. On the other hand the commands that are used to control the execution of BASIC programs vary considerably; those used in this book apply to the International Computers Ltd (ICL) 1900 and System 4 series of computers.

Most of the chapters that present elements of BASIC do so by first introducing a problem or case study. The method of solution of the problem is given in the form of a flow chart and the various statements of the BASIC language then arise naturally from the need to translate the flow chart into a computer program. The methods of solution are described briefly and, where appropriate, a suitable reference is given; details of the references can be found at the back of the book. After definitions of the new BASIC facilities required, the reader is usually presented with some brief exercises with which he can check his understanding of the material. Most of the chapters contain a second problem, sometimes used to illustrate refinements to the BASIC statements introduced earlier in the chapter; in the later chapters of the book these second problems are deliberately quite sophisticated, in the hope that they will challenge and interest the reader. The chapters conclude with some exercises on which the reader can practise his new-found knowledge; in each case a few straightforward problems are followed by some harder ones.

In most cases these programming exercises do not contain data for testing the programs, but the choice of such data is discussed in chapter 6. Nor do we usually specify that the programs should be run on a computer, though they presumably will be if at all possible since that is the only real way to progress.

To avoid the need for searching through the book for some particular detail of BASIC, all the elements of the language that are presented in the book are summarised on the front and back covers.

2 THE COMPUTER SYSTEM AND YOU

2.1 INTRODUCTION

An electronic computer is a piece of precision equipment like a
machine tool or a tape recorder. If it is manufactured, installed
and maintained properly, and instructed correctly, it will work as
it is designed to.

   There are essentially two types of electronic computer: analog
and digital. We shall only be concerned with digital computers.
These are rather like giant calculating machines: they can perform
all of the usual arithmetic operations, and at very high speeds.
As well as arithmetic calculations they are designed to be able to
store large amounts of information and to take logical decisions
based on the values of particular stored numbers. To instruct computers to perform all these operations we have to be able to communicate with them, and we achieve this by writing programs of
instructions using a computer language; this book aims to teach
the computer language called BASIC, which is acceptable to all the
major brands of computer.

   The advantages of using digital computers, compared with calculating by hand, are their very high speed, their stamina and their
accuracy. Computers break down like any other machinery, but when
they are working they almost never 'make a mistake'. The disadvantage of using these powerful machines is precisely that they
are machines. When human beings do calculations, intelligence and
intuition are used to make judgements about the progress of the
work; computers have no such ability and merely follow the instructions given to them, even if those instructions lead to answers
that are meaningless nonsense. One of the principal messages of
this book is that the output from computers is only as good as the
input of instructions and data allows them to be; this should always
be checked as far as possible. Hence the catchphrase: 'rubbish
in - rubbish out'.

2.2 THE COMPUTER SYSTEM

In the early days of computing the user went to the machine, pushed
buttons, fed in information punched on paper tape and collected
from it results on paper tape. The situation is rather more complicated than that now, but the user is protected from the compli-
cations by professional people who are responsible for running
computers. This section describes a typical complete computer
system and section 2.3 describes the main ways in which a user
interacts with such a system.

2.2.1 Hardware

The computer user does not need to know very much about the equipment that makes up a computer. An outline diagram of a typical system is shown in figure 2.1.

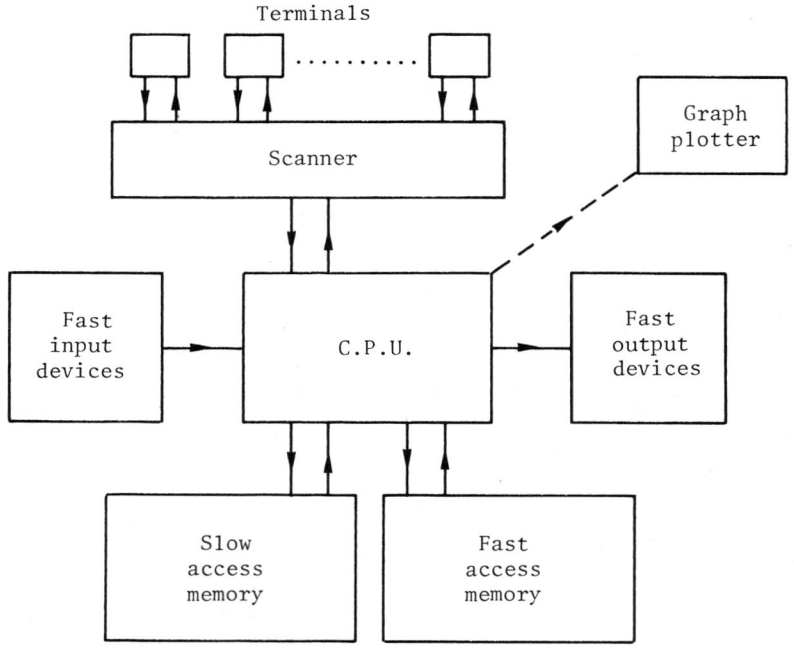

Fast input devices: card reader, paper tape reader.
Fast output devices: line printer, card punch, paper tape punch.
Slow access memory: magnetic tape, magnetic disk, magnetic drum.

Figure 2.1 Typical digital computer system

The Central Processing Unit (CPU) is the heart of the computer, controlling all the logical and organisational operations including transfer of data and instructions from the memory to the arithmetic unit (also in the CPU) and back, from input devices to the memory, and from the memory to the output devices.

The two types of memory shown in figure 2.1 are necessary because the fast-access type, which is used for all the actual processing of instructions and data, is very expensive. In most systems magnetic-disc storage is used to help out the fast-access memory when it is overloaded and to store information that is needed regularly, such as standard software (see section 2.2.2). Magnetic-tape storage on the other hand is used for longer-term storage. Of the input media, punched cards seem to be the most popular, but punched paper tape is quite common. Output is usually on to a line printer, so-called because it prints a line at a time (quite often at speeds over 1000 lines per minute). Output on punched cards or paper tape is usually only for subsequent reinput to the computer.

Graph plotters are very useful devices for engineers and scientists. They have a continuous roll of paper and a pen, which move in mutually perpendicular directions. These directions act as axes relative to which experimental results, computer solutions, etc., can be plotted for the usual reason that human beings understand such visual representations rather better than lists of figures. Graph plotters are relatively slow devices and are often run from information produced by the computer and stored on magnetic tape, rather than more directly by the computer.

Finally, terminals, which may be teletypewriters or visual display units based on cathode-ray tubes, are special input/output devices, and play an important role in this book. They are such that the user can type in messages directly to, and receive messages directly from, the computer. Such 'interactive working' is usually done with a 'conversational language', and BASIC is designed to be just such a language.

2.2.2 Software

A list of instructions that a computer system can accept and process is called a computer program. A modern computer system does not simply process the computer programs of users, it is actually organised by its own program, which is called an operating system. It is the operating system that will accept and organise the processing of programs, unless a very simple computer is used.

Computer programs are written at various levels. At the lowest level the instructions are written in machine code, which is the computer's own language. A machine-code program is usually a string of binary numbers telling the computer, for example, to move the contents of a storage location to the arithmetic unit, or other similarly basic operations. Operating systems may well be written in machine code.

One of the great steps forward in computing was the invention of computer languages that are easier to understand than machine code. The further the language is removed from machine code the easier it is to understand, and the harder it is for the computer to deal with. Nevertheless it is now established that these extra computer costs are acceptable in order to allow the casual user to write his own computer programs, and that is what this book is all about. All such high-level languages have to be translated by the computer itself into its own machine code, and this is done by further programs called compilers or interpreters. The compilers play another important role by checking the program that they are translating for obvious mistakes in syntax, such as spelling or punctuation, but they cannot of course guarantee beforehand that the program will produce the right answers.

Apart from providing an operating system and compilers for the various languages such as COBOL, FORTRAN, ALGOL and BASIC, the computer manufacturer will probably include in the total system prewritten packages for a wide variety of applications, from sewer design to the generation of random numbers. Some of these routines can be incorporated into the programs of users and some are complete programs in themselves.

2.2.3 Management

A large computer system is a very expensive investment and is likely to be run twenty-four hours a day. To achieve a reasonable benefit from such an investment it is usual to employ computer professionals to manage the system. They will include data preparation staff, who punch cards or paper tape from the users' instructions; computer operators, who feed the cards and paper tape to the machine, collect the output and generally superintend the day-to-day running of the system; computer programmers, who maintain the software, give advice to users, and perhaps write programs for them; and a computer manager to oversee all the above personnel, ensuring that the system as a whole achieves its object of providing a computer service to its users.

2.3 MODES OF OPERATION

There are essentially two different ways in which a user can cause the computer to process information from him: on-line and off-line. On-line working means that the user is actually in contact with the computer, usually through a terminal, inputting programs and data and receiving results; off-line working means that the user prepares his programs and data on a medium such as punched cards (or asks for them to be punched for him), presents these to the computer system through a receptionist, and collects the output from the receptionist at some later time. This delay could be minutes, hours or days, depending on the system.

In contrast, a terminal user working on-line to a well-designed system will appear to have virtually sole use of the computer. The reason that there are not more terminals is the relatively large amount of computer-processing power required to service them. For example, a system that is capable of servicing ten terminals simultaneously could, as an alternative, be running approximately five hundred off-line programs (depending on their size) in a twenty-four hour day. In practise this means that five hundred users could get a one-day turn-round from the system used off-line, whereas it is unlikely that those same people would each be able to satisfy their requirements from ten terminals, especially since most of us like working from 9 a.m. to 5 p.m. only!

Nevertheless, the interactive use of computer terminals is an increasingly important part of engineering design, the analysis of experimental data, and other similar activities, and most computer systems therefore use a mixture of on- and off-line working. The BASIC computer-programming language can be used in both modes, but we shall emphasise the on-line aspects because the language was designed to be used in that way.

3 PROBLEM SOLVING

3.1 WHO DOES WHAT

Perhaps the first surprise in store for the new user of computers is that these powerful machines do not in general *solve* anything. We cannot (yet) walk up to a computer and ask it to solve a problem that it has not been preprogrammed to recognise, because human beings have to decide *how* the problem should be solved; the computer is then used to do the labour of the calculations. The machine is quite simply a robot, which follows exactly and blindly the instructions given to it.

So the usual sequence of events is as follows.

(1) The person with the problem decides on the method of solution.
(2) They write a computer program that sets out logically and precisely the steps necessary to achieve the solution.
(3) They feed the program and the data to the computer which, all things being correct, produces the solution.

There are two major difficulties here. Firstly, it may be far from easy to decide on the best method of solution, and the fact that we are to use a computer for the calculations must be taken into account in the decision. Secondly, unless one is an experienced computer user, the task of unambiguously writing down the steps that make up the method of solution in such a way that a robot will obtain the answers by following those steps, will prove challenging at the very least. This chapter is concerned with that task. To illustrate these ideas we shall use as our main example the operation of interpolating in a table of data, starting with a simple version of the problem and moving on by two stages of development to a relatively sophisticated version. This problem and the three versions of its solution obtained in this chapter are used in chapters 4, 5 and 7 as examples of the need for the BASIC facilities introduced there

3.2 ALGORITHMS

The set of instructions that we translate into a computer program is called an algorithm. More precisely, an algorithm for a given problem is a sequence of instructions that unambiguously defines a method of obtaining a solution to the problem, if a solution exists, in a finite number of steps. If a solution does not exist the algorithm should 'fail safe', by indicating to the user that there is no solution.

As a very simple example, consider the solution of the equations

$$a_{11}x_1 + a_{12}x_2 = b_1$$
$$a_{21}x_1 + a_{22}x_2 = b_2$$
(3.1)

where x_1 and x_2 are the unknown quantities. By elementary algebra we find that

$$x_1 = \frac{b_1 a_{22} - b_2 a_{12}}{a_{11} a_{22} - a_{21} a_{12}}$$

$$x_2 = \frac{b_2 a_{11} - b_1 a_{21}}{a_{11} a_{22} - a_{21} a_{12}}$$
(3.2)

So we could instruct the computer as follows.

(1) Input values of a_{11}, a_{21}, a_{12}, a_{22}, b_1 and b_2.
(2) Calculate the values of x_1 and x_2.
(3) Output the values of x_1 and x_2.

But this would not be an algorithm in the strict sense of the word because instruction (2) would cause 'overflow' (the attempt to create a number larger than the largest number that the computer can store), if $a_{11}a_{22} - a_{21}a_{12} = 0$. We can create a proper algorithm by adding the extra instruction

(1a) If $a_{11}a_{22} - a_{21}a_{12} = 0$ then output 'no solution'.

In fact this still does not result in a completely useful computer algorithm.

The problem is that if we divide by a 'small' number we may have solutions just as nonsensical as those implied by trying to divide by zero. The reason for this is that, in practice, the data in our problems tend to be numbers with errors in them; these may be experimental errors or errors due to rounding infinite decimal numbers (like π and $\frac{1}{3}$). So, for example, $a_{11}a_{22} - a_{21}a_{12}$ might be small when it should be zero, and this could cause answers to be given when none actually exist.

A complete analysis of this kind of error problem, and the general study of methods of solving problems by computer, belongs to the subject of numerical mathematics. This subject is of great importance to engineers and scientists who are regularly involved in the analysis and synthesis of designs and experiments. One might say that to be able to write computer programs without knowing any numerical mathematics is like being able to operate a cooker without knowing any cookery recipes, so the reader is heartily advised to consult the references in this text to books giving details of the numerical methods used.

Returning to our algorithm, a more sensible way of writing down the extra instruction is

(1a) If $|a_{11}a_{22} - a_{21}a_{12}| < e$ then output 'no solution'.

where e is some predetermined tolerance that should be input with the other data. This at least gives the user some control over the errors that are produced. ($|x|$ means the absolute value, or magnitude, of x.)

3.3 FLOW CHARTS

Writing down the algorithm as a numbered sequence of instructions is quite valuable because it is then quite close to being a computer

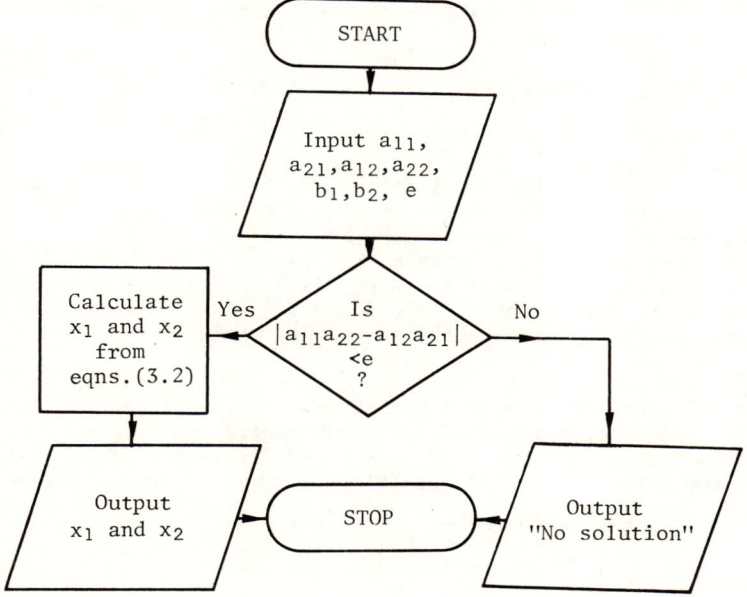

Figure 3.1(a)   Flow chart for simultaneous equations algorithm

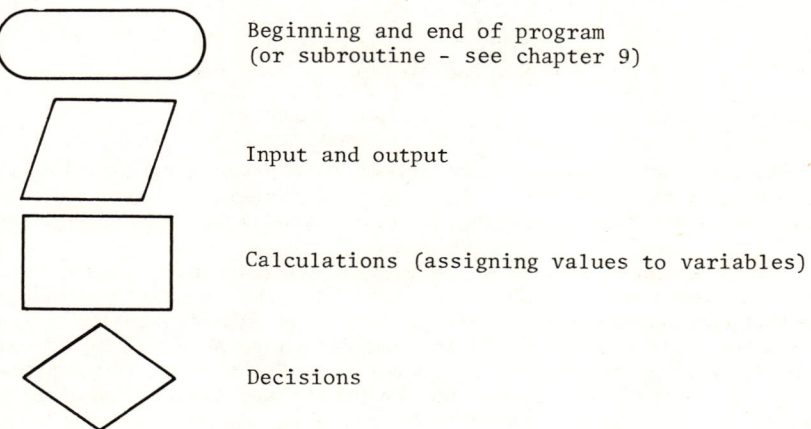

Figure 3.1(b)   Flow chart convention as used in this book

program; it simply has to be translated into the relevant computer language. Experience has shown, however, that it is somewhat easier to construct algorithms in the form of flow charts.

Figure 3.1 shows a flow chart for the solution of the simultaneous equations considered in section 3.1. Notice the convention of using different-shaped boxes for different operations.

A flow chart is also easier to read and alter than a numbered sequence of instructions. In each of the case studies used as examples in this book the algorithm used to solve the problem will be described by a flow chart.

3.4 CASE STUDY - LINEAR INTERPOLATION

Consider the problem of a manufacturer who wishes to publish a specification of the performance of some equipment that he has designed and is about to market. He has a choice of three ways of doing this: by a graph, a table or a formula. In each case the potential customer will want to interpolate in the data in order to evaluate the performance of the equipment for the particular operating conditions under which he wishes to use it.

Graphs are used when the accuracy of the information can be limited to about two significant figures. A typical example (figure 3.2) is the performance of pumps for central-heating systems. The system designer simply reads off a crude estimate of the volumetric flow rate for a given regulator setting and head of water.

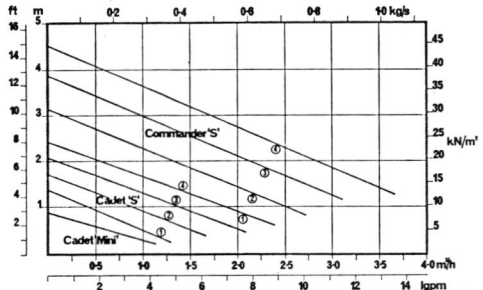

Figure 3.2 Circulating pump characteristics
(Sealed Motor Construction Co. Ltd.)

For more accurate communication of data a table or formula is used. If a table is given that does not contain the particular value required then an estimate of some kind will have to be made.

The same choice has to be made by a publisher of standard data. Typical graphical representations can be found in all the handbooks of the various engineering disciplines; for example, in *Reference Data for Radio Engineers* [1] the current-carrying capacity of various sizes of etched copper conductor as a function of temperature is given in graphical form. On the other hand typical tabular representations are given in standard tables of physical properties of fluids. For example, figure 3.3 shows a table of the specific heat capacity of saturated water and steam at given temperatures and corresponding pressures, so that if the user wants to know the specific heat capacities at, say, 175 °C then he has to estimate some value lying between 4.366 and 4.403 for water and between 2.504 and 2.615 for steam.

t °C	$p_s \times 10^{-5}$ N/m²	Water c_{pf} kJ/kg°C	Steam c_{pg} kJ/kg°C
0	0.0061	4.218	1.863
10	0.0123	4.194	1.870
20	0.0234	4.182	1.880
30	0.0424	4.179	1.890
40	0.0738	4.179	1.900
50	0.1233	4.181	1.912
60	0.1992	4.185	1.924
70	0.3116	4.191	1.946
80	0.4736	4.198	1.970
90	0.7011	4.207	1.999
100	1.0133	4.218	2.034
110	1.433	4.230	2.076
120	1.985	4.244	2.125
130	2.701	4.262	2.180
140	3.614	4.282	2.245
150	4.760	4.306	2.320
160	6.181	4.334	2.406
170	7.920	4.366	2.504
180	10.027	4.403	2.615
190	12.55	4.446	2.741
200	15.55	4.494	2.883
210	19.08	4.550	3.043
220	23.20	4.613	3.223
230	27.98	4.685	3.426
240	33.48	4.769	3.656
250	39.78	4.866	3.918
260	46.94	4.985	4.221
270	55.05	5.134	4.575
280	64.19	5.307	4.996
290	74.45	5.520	5.509
300	85.92	5.794	6.148
310	98.70	6.143	6.968
320	112.90	6.604	8.060
330	128.7	7.241	9.580
340	146.1	8.225	11.87
350	165.4	10.07	15.8
360	186.7	15.0	27.0
370	210.5	55	107
374.15	221.2	∞	∞

Figure 3.3 Specific heat capacity of saturated water and steam. (Engineering Sciences Data Item No. 68008 Table IV.)

Lastly, if a formula is given then the user has simply to substitute his operating conditions into the formula to calculate the performance figures required.

The choice between providing a table and a formula is a matter of convenience and, to some extent, prejudice. There have been instances where a simple formula exists and has been used to produce a table of data because the supplier thought that the potential customers would mistrust anything as mathematical as a formula. Similarly the published table of data may be produced by a computer program (new aircraft engines, for example, before prototypes have been made and tested) when a more sensible approach might be for the potential buyer to use the program to evaluate directly the performance figures he wants.

Nevertheless the use of tables to communicate values of functions, such as specific heat capacity as a function of temperature and pressure (figure 3.3), is likely to remain a widespread practice, and interpolation in such tables is the problem to which we now direct our attention. In particular we shall assume that the data are sufficiently densely tabulated for straight lines connecting adjacent data points to give sufficiently accurate values at the intermediate non-tabulated points. For example, if we plot the data from figure 3.3 for temperatures in steps of 50 °C (see figure 3.4) then it is intuitively clear that the estimate of the specific heat capacity of water when t = 175 °C is unlikely to be as accurate as the tabulated data itself. On the other hand (figure 3.5), if we plot the data for temperatures in steps of 10 °C, then it does seem reasonable to use a linear representation for the estimation of the same specific heat capacity. (This is why 10 °C was chosen as the spacing of the data.)

For a fuller discussion of this operation of linear interpolation, and its extension to quadratic and higher degree interpolation, the reader is advised to consult chapter 8 of Stark [2].

So the basic problem to be solved is: given two adjacent data points, say (x_1, y_1) and (x_2, y_2), estimate by linear interpolation the value of y for a given value of x satisfying $x_1 < x < x_2$. The answer is obtained by writing down the equation of the straight line joining the two points

$$y = y_1 + \frac{y_2 - y_1}{x_2 - x_1} (x - x_1) \qquad (3.3)$$

Thus the Mark 1 version of our linear-interpolation algorithm is as shown in the flow chart of figure 3.6.

Note that this is not an algorithm if $x_1 = x_2$; since this would only occur by mistake we shall not protect ourselves against it happening in this or the subsequent versions of the algorithm. This kind of compromise is quite usual in small-scale scientific computer programming; without it programs could be most unwieldy.

On the other hand we should check that $x_1 \leq x \leq x_2$, otherwise the algorithm would be misused. Although we shall not make such

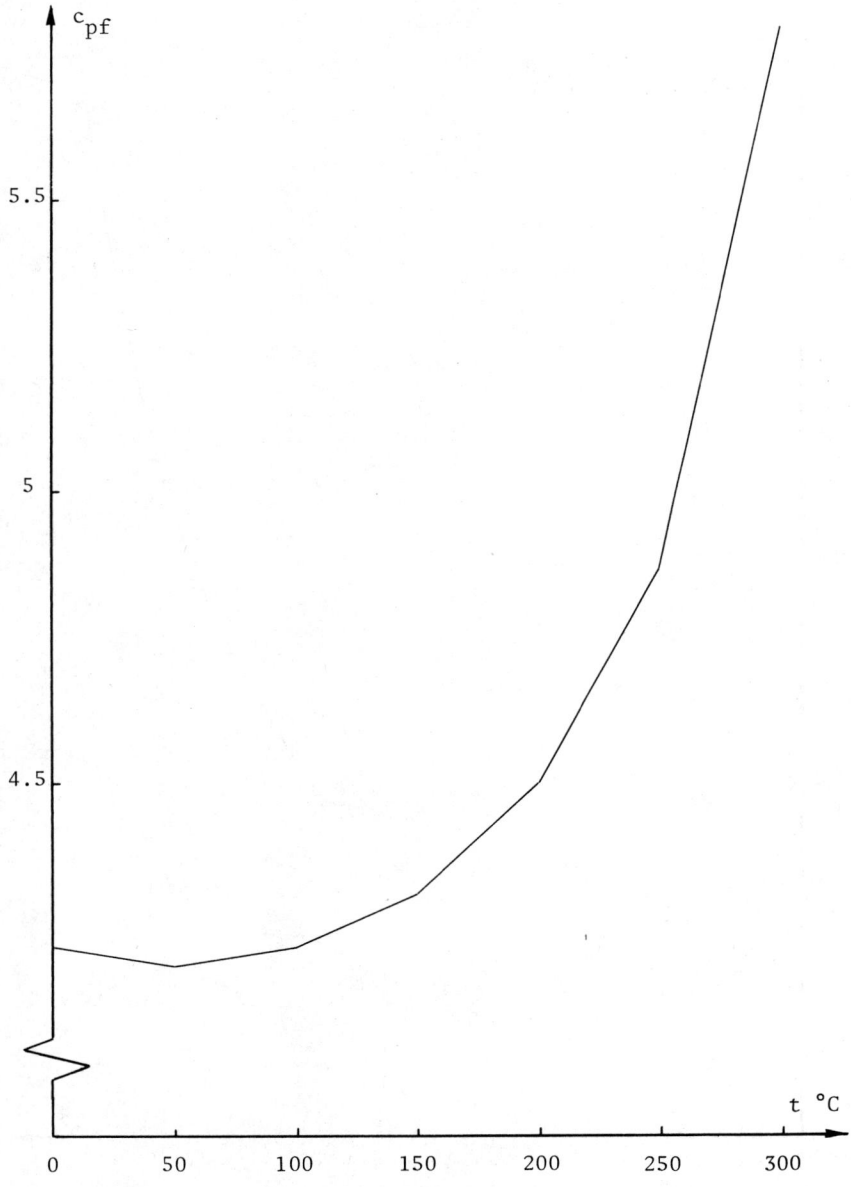

Figure 3.4 Polygonal approximation to c_{pf} (see figure 3.3) with temperature t in steps of 50°C

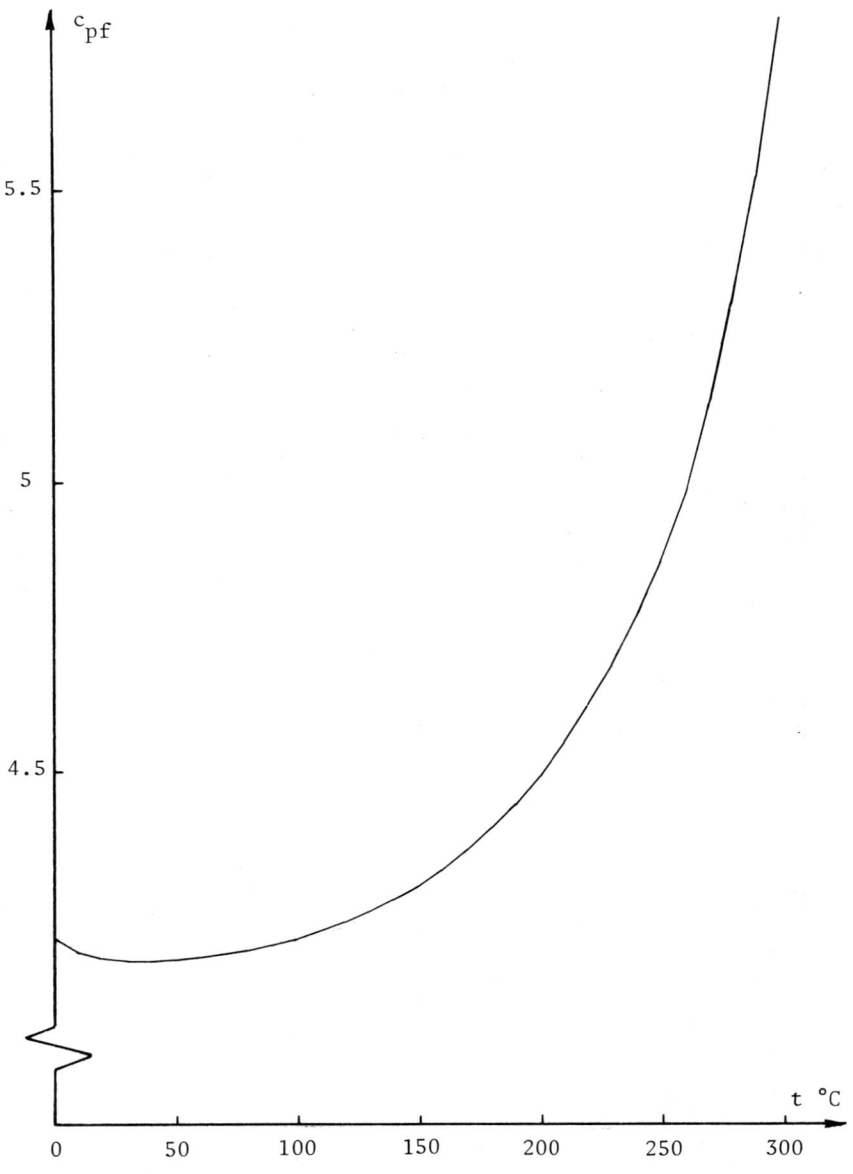

Figure 3.5 Polygonal approximation to c_{pf} (see figure 3.3) with temperature t in steps of 10°C

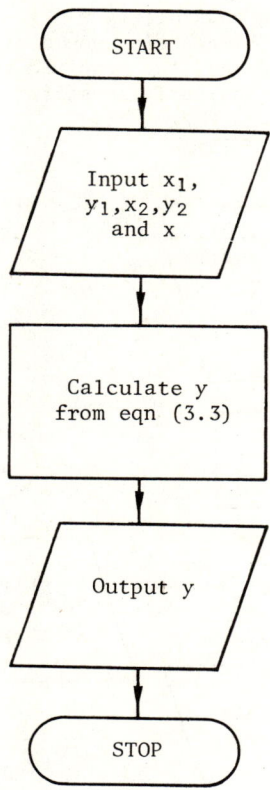

Figure 3.6 Flow chart for Mk. 1 linear interpolation algorithm

a check in this Mark 1 version (for a very good reason - it would then be unsuitable for use as an example in chapter 4), we shall incorporate a corresponding check in our Mark 2 version. (If $x = x_1$ or x_2 we would not normally do the calculation, because $y = y_1$ or y_2 respectively, but it would not be wrong to do so.)

3.5 AN IMPROVED LINEAR INTERPOLATION ALGORITHM

The algorithm of figure 3.6 is of course useless. We would not use a computer to do such a trivial calculation. The algorithm assumes that we have found the two data points (x_1, y_1) and (x_2, y_2) between which we wish to interpolate. As an intermediate stage between the trivial algorithm of figure 3.6 and the quite useful algorithm of section 3.7 let us construct one that does the search for the two relevant data points as well as the interpolation itself.

We shall suppose that we have n data points. Now consider: how should we instruct a robot to search through the data until two adjacent x values, x_1 and x_2, are such that $x_1 \leq x < x_2$? (Note that we have to include the possibility $x = x_1$ now that we are automating the process. A human being would simply observe that x was a tabulated value and read the required value of y from the table; the computer will laboriously substitute $x = x_1$ in equation 3.3 to produce $y = y_1$.)

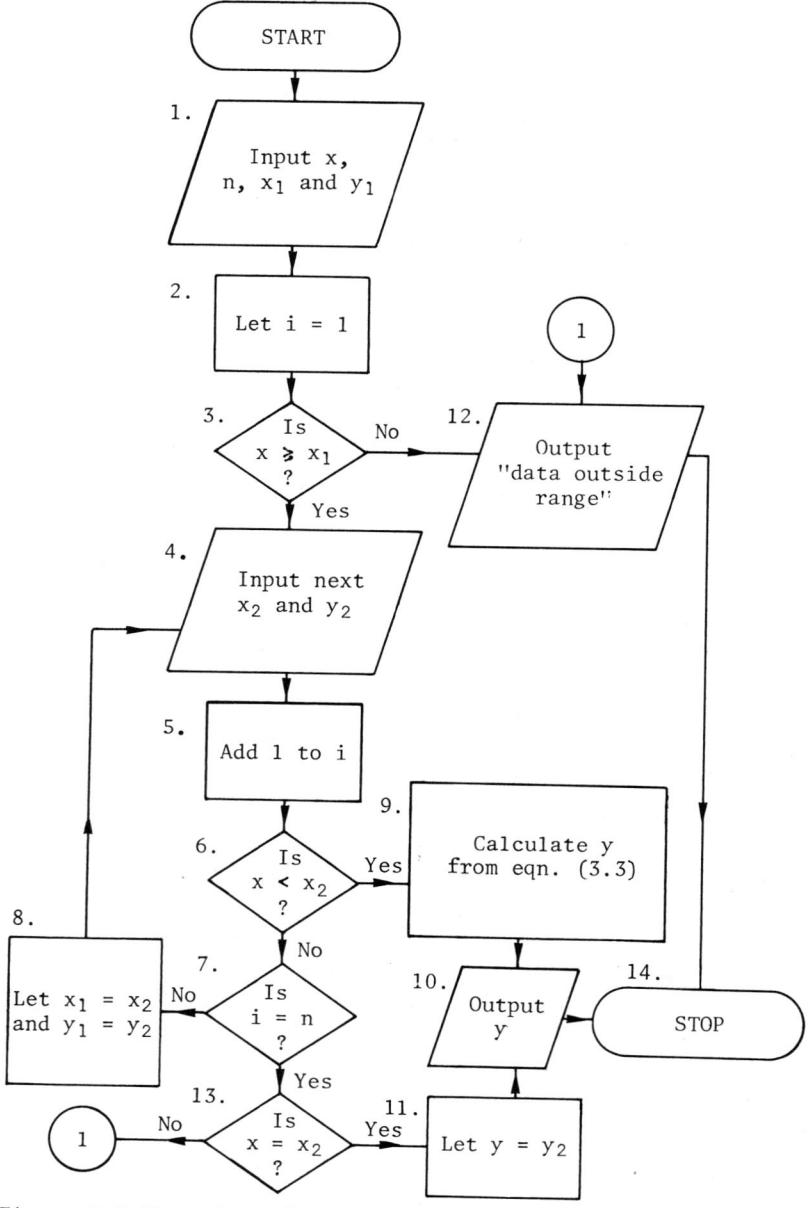

Figure 3.7 Flow chart for Mk. 2 linear interpolation algorithm

A simple answer is that we should instruct the computer to look at each tabulated value of x in turn (in increasing order) and ask if x is less than that value. If x is less than the first tabulated value then it is out of the range of the table, if it is not less than the first but is less than the second then we interpolate between the first and second, and so on. Finally we should have to check whether the given x value equalled the last tabulated x value. A flow chart for this algorithm is given in figure 3.7.

The really tremendous difference between this and our Mark 1 algorithm is the loop that effects the search for the interval $x_1 \leq x < x_2$ containing the given value of x. It is important to understand how the loop works: a counter i is established; it is given the value 1 initially (box 2) and is increased by 1 (box 5) each time a new data pair (x_2, y_2) is input; when i reaches the value n (box 7) we know that the data are exhausted. Note too that at any time (x_1, y_1) is the 'old' point and (x_2, y_2) the 'new', so that a swap is necessary (box 8) before the next 'new' point is input.

3.6   TRACE TABLES

The standard method of checking that an algorithm is correct is to work through it using data that test all its aspects. The result of each step is recorded in a trace table. Figure 3.8 shows a trace

Box No.	x	n	i	x_1	y_1	x_2	y_2	y	Decision	Output
1	2.5	4		1	1					
2			1							
3									No	
4						2	4			
5			2							
6									No	
7									No	
8				2	4					
4						3	7			
5			3							
6									Yes	
9								5.5		
10										5.5

Figure 3.8   Trace table for Mk. 2 linear interpolation algorithm

table for the flow chart of figure 3.7. The table of data used is as follows.

x	1	2	3	4
y	1	4	7	10

We have tested the algorithm by interpolating at x = 2.5, that is, in the centre of the table. To test fully we should use data that can distinguish whether the algorithm has *all* the properties required of it. The reader is advised first to make sure that he can follow the construction of figure 3.8, and then to construct his own trace tables for the other three main possibilities: x to the left of the table, x at the right-hand end of the table and x to the right of the table (for example, x = 0, x = 4 and x = 5).

3.7 A FURTHER IMPROVED LINEAR INTERPOLATION ALGORITHM

In the Mark 2 version of our algorithm we deliberately avoided storing the whole table of data in the computer by inputting each point in turn, subsequently discarding a previous point, so that at any one time only two adjacent data points were stored. This is fine if only one interpolation is to be made. If, however, we need to evaluate y for many values of x then we should avoid inputting the data more than once.

Let the data points be called (x_1, y_1), (x_2, y_2), ..., (x_n, y_n) and suppose we need to interpolate for m different values of x (not necessarily in any particular order). Figure 3.9 shows a flow chart for this Mark 3 linear interpolation algorithm. Compare it carefully with figure 3.7. Note in particular the new way in which the loops are indicated [i = 1(1)n means i takes the values 1 to n in steps of 1]. The circles are simply junction boxes.

Note that we have had to rewrite equation 3.3 to perform interpolation between x_{i-1} and x_i, instead of between x_1 and x_2. To ensure that he understands how this version works, the reader should construct a trace table using the same data that were used in section 3.6, that is, the table there plus m = 4, and x = 2.5, 0, 4 and 5 in turn.

3.8 POSTSCRIPT

If this chapter was found to be quite difficult, then remember the warning of section 3.2: the construction of algorithms is not easy until quite considerable experience of doing it has been gained.
It is quite straightforward now to read on into the first few chapters on BASIC programming, because the flow charts of this chapter will be used as examples. But remember that, in general, the problem will need to be analysed, and an algorithm constructed, before programming the method for the computer.

EXERCISES

3.1 Draw a flow chart for an algorithm that finds the real roots

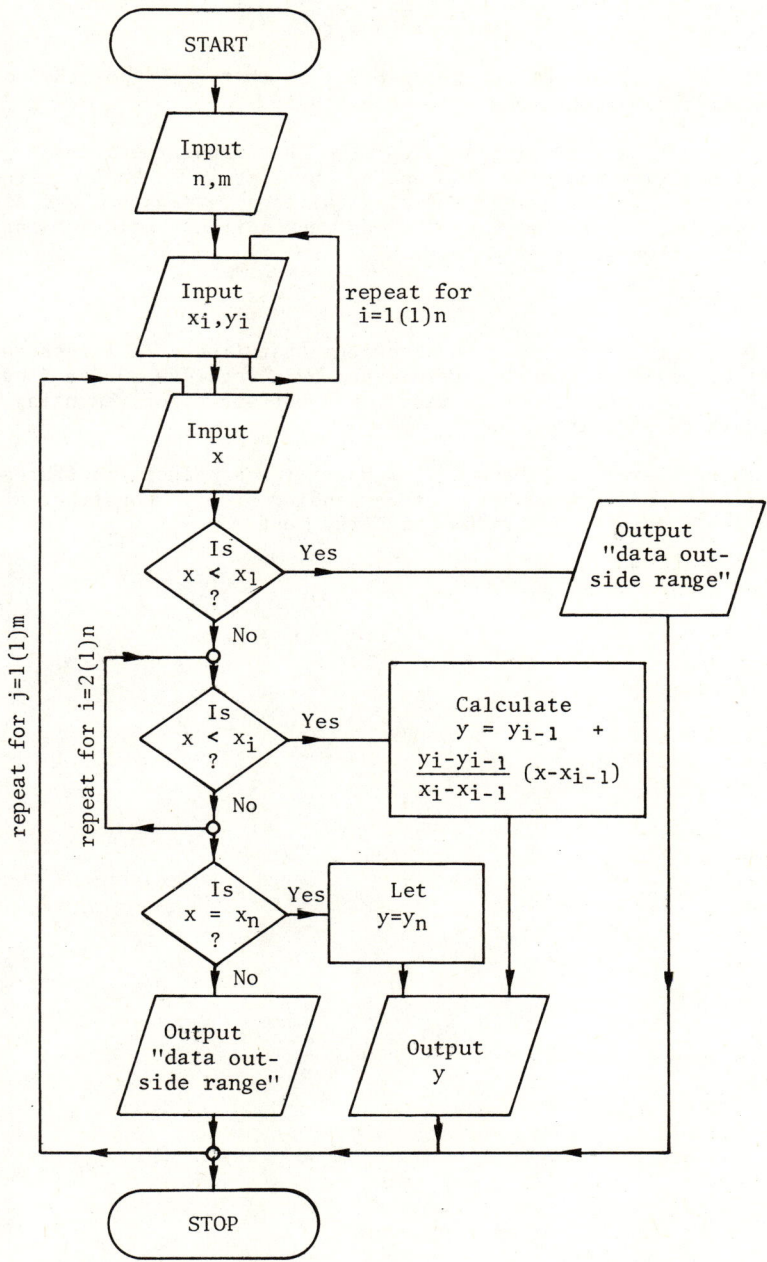

Figure 3.9 Flow chart for Mk. 3 linear interpolation algorithm

of the quadratic equation $ax^2 + bx + c = 0$. The algorithm should output a message if the roots are not real.

3.2 Modify your answer to exercise 3.1 so that the algorithm solves n quadratic equations, one after the other.

3.3 Draw a flow chart for an algorithm that finds the average of a list of positive numbers. The end of the list is to be indicated by a single negative number (usually called a terminator, and not to be included in the average). Construct a trace table for the algorithm using the test data.

    1, 9, 5, -1

3.4 Draw a flow chart for an algorithm that finds the largest of a list of positive numbers, terminated by a negative number (see exercise 3.3). Construct a trace table for the algorithm using the test data of exercise 3.3.

3.5 (Harder exercise) Draw a flow chart for an algorithm that sorts a list of n positive numbers into ascending order. Construct a trace table for the algorithm using the test data.

    5, 9, 1, 3

4 BASIC - THE FIRST ESSENTIALS

4.1 CASE STUDY - LINEAR INTERPOLATION MARK 1

To help introduce the fundamental elements of BASIC we shall use the Mark 1 version of the linear interpolation algorithm (see section 3.3). In particular we shall refer quite often to the flow chart given in figure 3.6.

4.2 *BASIC* REQUIREMENTS

Since this is the first chapter on BASIC there will be rather more new ideas to understand than will be the case in later chapters. On the other hand all the ideas in this chapter are quite elementary.

If we study figure 3.6 we see that any computer language capable of instructing a computer to perform the algorithm must be able to command the machine to

(1) accept the program
(2) start execution of the program
(3) input data values and associate them with named variables
(4) calculate the value of an arithmetic expression and associate the value with a named variable
(5) output the values of named variables
(6) stop the program
(7) terminate working in BASIC.

Implicit in many of the above are the ideas of numerical data values and variables. We shall deal with these first and then return to the list above.

4.2.1 Numeric constants and variables

A numeric constant can be written in two ways in BASIC.

(a) As a 'fixed point' number, for example

    15.31
    0
    -0.01234
    -20

(The maximum possible number of digits varies between computer systems, but since the output is usually given to six significant figures it is not sensible to use numbers that are much more accurate.)

(b) As a 'floating-point' number, for example

    1.531E1, meaning 15.31
    -1.234E-2, meaning -0.01234

In general, mEn, where m is a fixed-point number and n is a positive or negative two-digit integer (whole number), means $m \times 10^n$. This form is most useful for representing very large and very small numbers, for example

1E-6 means 0.000001
5.6E8 means 560 000 000

Numeric variables will, at any instant in time during the execution of a program, have some (constant) value, but the value can be changed during that execution. These variables thus play the same role in BASIC as variables do in algebra. A simple way of thinking of numeric variables in a computer program is as labels for pigeon-holes in which numbers are stored. In the Mark 1 version of the linear interpolation algorithm we need six pigeon-holes, one each for x_1, y_1, x_2, y_2, x and y. (See figure 4.1 where typical values have been stored.)

x_1	y_1	x_2	y_2	x	y
2	4	3	7	2.5	5.5

Figure 4.1 Storage of variables for Mk. 1 algorithm

In BASIC variables such as these can have one of 286 possible names. These are

A, A0, A1, ..., A9, B, B0, B1, ..., B9, ..., Z, Z0, ..., Z9

that is, a single capital letter, or a single capital letter followed by a single numeric digit. So we have no problem for our case study, we can use the variables X1, Y1, X2, Y2, X and Y.

4.2.2 NEW OR OLD?

Returning to our list of requirements, the first one was the need to be able to instruct the computer to accept a program. Such an instruction is called a command in BASIC and is not part of the program itself. (BASIC commands vary considerably between computer systems and it is worth recalling the statement in section 1.2 that the commands given in this book are those required by ICL System 4 and 1900 series computers.)

When a computer system is activated from a terminal to be receptive to BASIC programs, the machine will print the message

NEW OR OLD?

on the terminal. In order to be able to type in a program the user replies to the above question by typing NEW followed by a space and then a suitable name for the program. For our case study we might type

NEW LINTERPMK1

At this point we must discuss briefly the practicalities of using a terminal. Terminals vary in design, but they all have a typewriter layout for the alphabet, numbers and punctuation marks. Apart from those symbols only two keys really interest us: there will be a key (usually labelled ACCEPT) that causes a line of typing to be transmitted to the computer; and there will be a key or keys that facilitate breaking in and stopping a program that is being executed (if, for example, it is clear that the execution is going wrong for some reason). Finally it should be realised that nothing can be typed until the computer invites it. This will be indicated by a symbol (for example, ←), which will therefore appear at the beginning of each line of typing.

We have said in a previous chapter that compilers are designed to recognise mistakes in BASIC statements and commands. If a line is mistyped, or anything that is not acceptable to the compiler is typed, the compiler will reply with some kind of message indicating the mistake. At the next invitation to type simply type the correct version of the incorrect line. Here is an example of a 'conversation' that could ensue between the computer and its user.

```
NEW OR OLD?
← NEW PROG 1
? NEW/
← NEW PROG1
← etc.
```

At the first attempt at the NEW command the user forgot that there must not be a space in the program name - usually only letters and numbers are allowed in program names. After typing the NEW command we can type in the whole program (when we have written it!). You will have guessed from the question NEW OR OLD? that there is an OLD command. It will be described in a later chapter.

4.2.3 RUN and BYE

The second requirement of our list in section 4.2 is to be able to start the program running. This is achieved by the command

    RUN

This is typed *after* the program is typed in.

The last requirement of our list is for a command that tells the computer that we have finished working in BASIC. This command is

    BYE

So a typical 'job' at a computer terminal would proceed as follows.

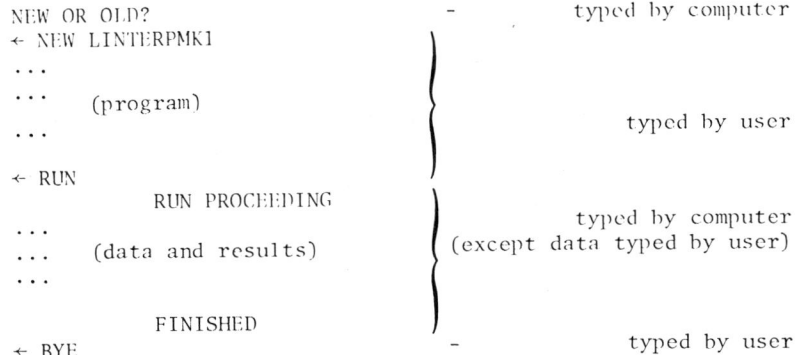

The messages RUN PROCEEDING and FINISHED are not universal but most systems will have similar indications of the beginning and end of a RUN.

4.2.4 Input of data

NEW, RUN and BYE are commands. We now introduce our first BASIC statement, that is, a statement that will be a part of a BASIC program, rather than a command to do something with the program.

In response to requirement (3) of section 4.2 we need a statement that causes input of data values for variables. There are two ways of doing this in BASIC as follows.

(1) If it is reasonable to prepare the data in advance we use a READ statement and the data are typed in a DATA statement. We separate by commas the variables in the READ statement and similarly the corresponding numbers in the DATA statement. For our case study (see figure 3.6) we might have

    READ X1,Y1,X2,Y2,X
    DATA 2,4,3,7,2.5

Note that there is no comma after the last entry in either list. The DATA statement can appear anywhere in a program since it is not actually executed.

(2) If we would prefer to input the data during the execution of the program (which we shall do in general) we use an INPUT statement. For example

    INPUT X1,Y1,X2,Y2,X

When the program is run, and when execution reaches the INPUT statement, the computer requests (by ← again, or perhaps by a question mark) the values of the variables indicated. The user then types the values, again separated by commas, but without the word DATA.

4.2.5 Arithmetic expressions and assignment statements

Requirement (4) involves the essence of the computer: its arithmetic capability. All computer languages for scientific (as opposed to commercial) use allow the programmer to write expressions in a form closely allied to the algebra that we normally use. The operation signs are almost all familiar to us

+ addition   (e.g. X1 + 1)
- subtraction   (e.g. 4 - W)
* multiplication   (e.g. 3.1416*A)
/ division   (e.g. 10/R)
** exponentiation   (e.g. B**(-3), meaning B^{-3})
  (raising to a power)

We can use brackets, again like ordinary algebra, to form quite complicated expressions, which are only limited in BASIC by the fact that each statement must be contained in a single typed line (normally seventy-five characters).

The arithmetic expression required in our case study is the one on the right of the equals sign in equation 3.3 (repeated here)

$$y = y_1 + \frac{y_2 - y_1}{x_2 - x_1} (x - x_1)$$

In BASIC it could be written

    Y1+(Y2-Y1)*(X-X1)/(X2-X1)

Here is a situation where we have to remember that the computer is a robot. We can be quite imprecise in algebra and expect to be understood. For example, the expression a/bc would normally be interpreted as a/(bc) because if we meant (a/b)c we would write ac/b. We have to be more precise in computer programming, and we would write

    A/(B*C)

In fact the computer will evaluate an expression by doing the operations in the following order (starting with the innermost brackets and working outwards)

(1) **
(2) * and /
(3) + and -

In a sequence of operations of equal rank the calculations are done from the left, so

    A/B*C

does indeed produce the same answer as

    (A/B)*C

just as we anticipated in the discussion above.

Arithmetic expressions appear in various situations. The one we are interested in at the moment is that in which its value is to be assigned to a certain variable. This is achieved by the assignment statement LET.

For our case study (see figure 3.6) we have

LET Y=Y1+(Y2-Y1)*(X-X1)/(X2-X1)

The value assigned to Y in this way replaces any previous value Y might have had.

A rather peculiar consequence of this replacement operation is that it is quite reasonable to write

LET N=N+1

which simply means: take the value of N, add 1 to it, and let the result be the new value of N; that is, in effect, add 1 to N.

The assignment statement is also used for the simple jobs of giving a variable an initial value, for example

LET X=0

and of transferring the value of one variable to another, for example

LET A=B

In other words, 0 and B are perfectly valid (if exceedingly simple) expressions that can be evaluated and then assigned.

Finally note that it is not allowable either to have two operators together, so A*-B should be written -A*B [or A*(-B) if you prefer], or to raise a negative number to a power unless that power is an integer.

4.2.6 Output of results

In contrast to the input of data, the output of results is quite complicated. Consequently we shall spread the details over two chapters: in this chapter the bare essentials and little more, in the next chapter the complete story.

All output is achieved by the PRINT statement. To PRINT the values of variables we simply list the variables, separated by commas. For reasons that we shall explain in the next chapter it is advisable to restrict the output of numbers to five per line.

For our case study (see figure 3.6) we need only

PRINT Y

but we shall see in sections 4.5 and 4.6 that we can improve on this rather bare statement.

4.2.7 END

Our last requirement is the stopping of the program. This is achieved by the END statement, which also serves to indicate the physical end of the program (that is, it is always the last statement in the program).

4.2.8 Line numbers

We are now nearly ready to write down a BASIC program for our case study. The only missing requirement, one that does not stem directly from the flow chart but is an intrinsic part of BASIC, is for each line of the program to be numbered in sequence. The usefulness of this numbering will become clear in a later chapter when we consider altering and inserting statements. To facilitate the introduction of extra statements it is normal to number in steps of 10. The first statement may have any line number.

Not only is the program executed in the order given by the line numbers but, for example, if there is more than one DATA statement then they are also used in sequence, according to their line numbers.

4.3 A PROGRAM FOR THE CASE STUDY

Collecting together all the bits and pieces, and adding one extra statement, we have the program shown in figure 4.2. Note that the NEW, RUN and BYE commands do not have line numbers, not being part of the program.

```
        NEW OR OLD?
     ← NEW LINTERPMK1
     ← 100 REM LINEAR INTERPOLATION, MK. 1
     ← 110 INPUT X1,Y1,X2,Y2,X
     ← 120 LET Y=Y1+(Y2-Y1)*(X-X1)/(X2-X1)
     ← 130 PRINT Y
     ← 140 END
     ←
        RUN
                    RUN PROCEEDING

     ← 2,4,3,7,2.5
        5.5

                    FINISHED
```

Figure 4.2 Program for Mk. 1 linear interpolation algorithm

The extra statement (100) is a REMark statement. It is ignored by the computer and is used by the programmer to store information about the program, either for himself or for another user. Like DATA statements, REMarks can appear anywhere in a program.

4.4 CHECK YOUR PROGRESS

To check the understanding of the material in section 4.2 and its subsections, try the following exercises.

(1) Which of the following are valid BASIC variable names?

(a) Q
(b) Q2
(c) 2Q
(d) QQ
(e) Q*

(2) Write down BASIC expressions corresponding to these algebraic expressions

(a) ab/c
(b) $a + \dfrac{b}{c}$
(c) $\dfrac{a + b}{c}$
(d) $\dfrac{a + b}{c + d}$
(e) $x^2 + 2X + 3$
(f) $\sqrt[5]{x - y}$
(g) $\sqrt{b^2 - 4ac}$

3. What will be the output from the following program?

```
10 READ P1,P2,N
20 DATA -6.7,-6.8,5
30 LET A=(P1+P2)/N
40 LET A=A*A
50 PRINT A
60 END
```

Answers

(1) (a) and (b) only. Remember: a variable name can be a letter, or a letter followed by a numeric digit, and nothing else.

(2) (a) A*B/C
(b) A+B/C
(c) (A+B)/C
(d) (A+B)/(C+D)
(e) X*X+2*X+3   (X*X is computed more quickly than X**2)
(f) (X-Y)**0.2
(g) (B*B-4*A*C)**0.5

(3) The output will be the number

   7.29

4.5 A SECOND CASE STUDY - THE AREA OF A TRIANGLE

The main purpose of our second example is to introduce the idea of 'strings'. A string is a sequence of characters, that is, numbers, letters and punctuation marks. The most common use of strings is for the clarification of output. For example, the output from LINTERPMK1 would be better if it said

Y=5.5 WHEN X=2.5

instead of the solitary number

5.5

To introduce the use of strings we shall consider the simple problem of calculating the area of a triangle when the lengths a, b and c of its three sides are given. There is a standard formula for the area q which is

$$q = \sqrt{[s(s - a)(s - b)(s - c)]} \quad (4.1)$$

where $2s = a + b + c$.

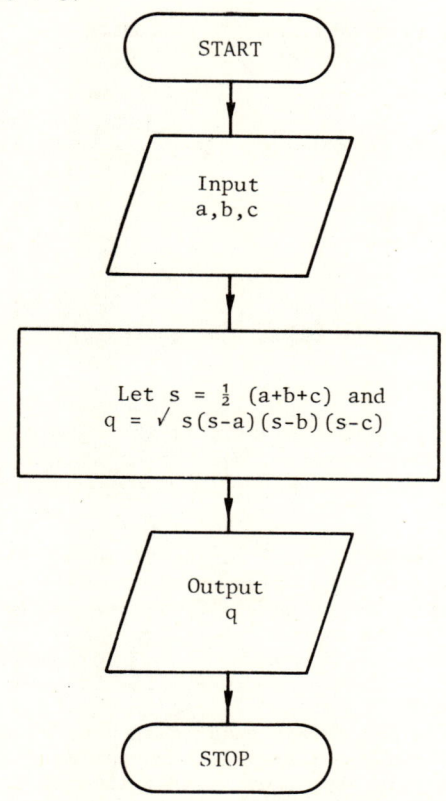

```
           ┌─────────┐
           │  START  │
           └────┬────┘
                │
           ┌────▼────┐
          /  Input   /
         /  a,b,c   /
        └──────────┘
                │
       ┌────────▼────────┐
       │ Let s = ½(a+b+c)│
       │ and             │
       │ q = √s(s-a)(s-b)(s-c) │
       └────────┬────────┘
                │
           ┌────▼────┐
          /  Output  /
         /     q    /
        └──────────┘
                │
           ┌────▼────┐
           │  STOP   │
           └─────────┘
```

Figure 4.3 Flow chart for calculating triangular area

So a flow chart for this calculation is very simple and is shown in figure 4.3. Before translating this into a BASIC program let us decide how we would like the output to appear. It is very good policy to print out the data (for future reference), so perhaps we should design the output thus

AREA OF TRIANGLE WITH SIDES OF LENGTH
<u>A</u> <u>B</u> <u>C</u> UNITS
IS <u>Q</u> SQUARE UNITS

where the quantities underlined are replaced by actual values when the program is run. To achieve this output we need the concept of a string.

4.6 STRINGS

A string is simply a list of BASIC characters (that is, those characters acceptable in BASIC).

4.6.1 String constants

A string constant is established by enclosing the relevant string in double quote marks. For example

"AREA OF TRIANGLE WITH SIDES"
"METRES"
"X ="
"GEORGE WASHINGTON"
"INPUT 1,2,3, OR 4"

In a particular case (see below) the quotes can be omitted.

4.6.2 String variables

A string variable is simply a variable whose 'value' is a string. There are usually twenty-six string variable names

A$, B$, C$, ..., Z$

In some versions of BASIC the $ can be £, in which case A$ and A£ refer to precisely the same 'pigeon-hole'. We shall use £ in this book. Another variation among BASIC systems is that some of them allow 286 names, as for numeric variables

A$, A1$, A2$, ..., A9$, ..., Z$, Z1$, ..., Z9$

String variables can be manipulated in many of the ways that numeric variables can be; the obvious exception is that one cannot normally do arithmetic with them. The following statements illustrate the possibilities for input, output and assignment.

```
100 LET A£="YES"
110 READ B£,N
120 DATA A.N.OTHER,23
130 PRINT "SALESMAN NO.",N,"IS",B£
140 PRINT "ANSWER YES OR NO"
150 INPUT C£
```

The output from line 130 would be

SALESMAN NO. 23 IS A.N.OTHER

except that the spacing would not be as neat as this. The details of the spacing of output are given in chapter 5. The output from lines 140 and 150 would be

ANSWER YES OR NO
←

the left-facing arrow being the computer's invitation to the user to type YES or NO for input into the string variable C£.

Note that the string in line 120, which was read into B£ by line 110, is not in quotes. This is the exception mentioned earlier. Similarly, the user's response to the ← above could be YES or NO, rather than "YES" or "NO". A string in quotes is called a closed string, and one without quotes an open string. Open strings can be used only as input data, that is, in a DATA statement or when responding to a request for input during program execution. Generally no string should contain quote marks - for obvious reasons - and an open string must not contain any commas. For example

DATA J.SMITH,ESQ.

will be interpreted as two strings, and should be written

DATA "J.SMITH,ESQ."

if one string is intended. Similarly if the first character of a string is a space, plus sign or minus sign then the string must be written in closed form.

Normally, there is a restriction on the number of characters allowed in one string - a common figure is fifteen characters. We shall not say anything about dealing with the problem of larger strings since this does not arise very often in scientific computing.

4.7 A PROGRAM FOR THE AREA OF A TRIANGLE

We can now translate into BASIC the flow chart of figure 4.3 in such a way that the output is as described at the end of section 4.5. The program is shown in figure 4.4. Work through this program line by line checking how the statements produce the output shown. In particular note the mixture of constant and variable strings such as "SQUARE" and L£, the latter storing "METRES" in this particular case.

```
NEW OR OLD?
← NEW TRIAREA
← 100 REM TRIANGLE AREA CALC.
← 110 PRINT "INPUT LENGTHS OF SIDES"
← 120 INPUT A,B,C
← 130 PRINT "WHAT UNITS OF LENGTH ARE YOU USING?"
← 140 INPUT L£
← 150 PRINT "AREA OF TRIANGLE WITH SIDES OF LENGTH"
← 160 PRINT A,B,C,L£
← 170 LET S=0.5*(A+B+C)
← 180 LET Q=(S*(S-A)*(S-B)*(S-C))**0.5
← 190 PRINT "IS",Q,"SQUARE",L£
← 200 END
←
  RUN
              RUN PROCEEDING
INPUT LENGTHS OF SIDES
← 3,4,5
WHAT UNITS OF LENGTH ARE YOU USING?
← METRES
AREA OF TRIANGLE WITH SIDES OF LENGTH
  3              4              5              METRES
IS               6.             SQUARE         METRES

            FINISHED
```

Figure 4.4   Program for calculation of triangular area

We shall use strings consistently throughout this book to clarify output and to input (and subsequently output) relevant alphanumeric (that is, not purely numeric) information.

EXERCISES

4.1 Rewrite the LINTERPMK1 program given in section 4.3 so that the output is as suggested at the beginning of section 4.5.

4.2 Write a BASIC program to input a positive number, and to output its square and square root in the form

    NO.= ...
    SQUARE= ...
    SQ. ROOT= ...

4.3 Write a BASIC program that inputs the radius of a circle and calculates and outputs its area and circumference. The output should include the radius and should be explained by the output of suitable strings.

4.4 Write a BASIC program that calculates and outputs the mass flow
$$M = A_1 A_2 [2\rho P/(A_1^2 - A_2^2)]^{\frac{1}{2}}$$

where A_1 and A_2 are cross-sectional areas, ρ is fluid density and P is pressure drop.

4.5 Write a BASIC program to solve a pair of simultaneous linear equations. Formulae for the solutions are given in equations 3.2. (At the end of chapter 5 you will be able to improve the program to deal with the failure possibilities discussed in section 3.1.)

5 BASIC - LOOPS AND BRANCHES

5.1 CASE STUDY - LINEAR INTERPOLATION MARK 2

In this chapter we shall be referring continuously to figure 3.7 - the flow chart for the Mark 2 linear interpolation algorithm. To make this easier the figure is repeated in section 5.3, near the corresponding BASIC program (figure 5.1).

If the Mark 2 algorithm's flow chart is compared with that for the Mark 1 version (figure 3.6) it will be seen that the main difference between them is that the Mark 1 version is 'linear', whereas the Mark 2 version is 'branching'. A branch in an algorithm is a point at which the natural sequence of events is interrupted and control is transferred to an instruction other than the immediately succeeding one.

For example, in figure 3.7, the BASIC instruction for box 10 cannot follow both that for box 9 and that for box 11. Therefore some kind of jump statement is required. A somewhat different branch occurs at boxes 3, 6, 7 and 13 where, in each case, the direction that the algorithm takes depends on a decision.

Perhaps the most important use to which the branching statements are put is the construction of loops. Recalling our discussion of the Mark 2 algorithm in section 3.5, we stressed this fact; indeed it is the concept that makes the Mark 2 version non-trivial when compared with the Mark 1, enabling it to search through the data to find the interval within which the interpolation is to be effected. The loop consists of boxes 4, 5, 6, 7 and 8 in figure 3.7, and it is box 7, the decision box, that controls the loop.

5.2 *BASIC* REQUIREMENTS

The two types of branch mentioned in the previous section have special names. The one that occurs as a result of a YES/NO decision is called a conditional branch; the other, the simple jump from one point in a program to another, is called an unconditional branch. The BASIC statements that achieve these branching operations are described in the next two subsections.

5.2.1 The unconditional branch statement - GO TO

This is a very simple statement. Its general form is

    GO TO line no.

where line no. is the line number of any executable statement in the program (that is, not a REMark, or DATA, or any other statement which only gives information).

For example, for boxes 9, 10 and 11 in figure 3.7 we may have statements such as

```
(box 9)    300 LET Y= ...
           310 GO TO 410
           ..........
(box 11)   400 LET Y=Y2
(box 10)   410 PRINT Y
(box 14)   420 END
```

A similar situation arises at box 12, which has to be connected to box 14. For example

```
(box 12)   200 PRINT "DATA OUTSIDE RANGE"
           210 GO TO 420
```

where line 420 is as shown above.

5.2.2 The conditional branch statement - IF ... THEN ...

The general form of this statement is

   IF proposition THEN line no.

where line no. is as described above for GO TO. The effect of this statement is to transfer control to the line number given after THEN if the proposition is true, and to allow execution to continue at the line after the IF ... THEN ... statement if the proposition is false.

The propositions that are allowed in BASIC are simple when compared with those of more sophisticated computer languages, but they are sufficient in the sense that more complicated situations can be dealt with by a sequence of IF ... THEN ... statements. Here are the allowable propositions; in each case A and B can be any arithmetic expression or string.

Proposition	Meaning
A = B	A equals B
A < > B	A does not equal B
A > B	A is greater than B
A > = B	A is greater than or equal to B
A < B	A is less than B
A < = B	A is less than or equal to B

When A and B are numeric less than and greater than are used in the usual algebraic sense so that, for example, -3 < 1 and -3 > -5. When A and B are strings the order of the characters depends on the computer being used, but in all systems A < B < C ... < Z and 0 < 1 < 2 ... < 9 (treated as characters, *not* numbers). For example, PQR < PQS and PQR > PQQ. We shall not pursue this ordering of strings because it does not arise very often in scientific work, but we shall occasionally use the more obvious comparisons for equality or non-equality. For example

    IF A£="YES" THEN 900
    IF P£<> Q£ THEN 225

In the second case a jump to line 225 occurs if the strings P£ and Q£ are not the same.

As examples of the comparison of numeric quantities consider the branches at boxes 6, 7 and 13 in figure 3.7.

(box 12)	200 PRINT "DATA OUTSIDE RANGE"
	....
(box 6)	250 IF X<X2 THEN 300
(box 7)	260 IF I=N THEN 320
	....
(box 9)	300 LET Y= ...
	310 GO TO 410
(box 13)	320 IF X<>X2 THEN 200
(box 11)	400 LET Y=Y2
(box 10)	410 PRINT Y
(box 14)	420 END

Note first how directly the decision boxes 6 and 7 translate into BASIC. Then look at how the line number connections match the box connections in the flow chart. Lastly note that, because of the position of box 12 as line 200, it is necessary to translate box 13 as though it were 'Is x not equal to x_2?', with the YES and NO outlets switched. All decision boxes can be 'negated' in this way. In practice we write whichever form of proposition we prefer in the flow chart, and then negate it if necessary when we write the computer program.

5.3 A PROGRAM FOR THE CASE STUDY

We are now able to write a program for the Mark 2 algorithm (figure 3.7 - repeated here). In fact we have constructed much of it in our examples of the GO TO and IF ... THEN ... statements.

Such a program and its execution for one of the data suggested in section 3.6 are shown in figure 5.1. Note how inefficient it would be to have to re-enter data to achieve interpolates at various values of x. This drawback is overcome by the Mark 3 version of the algorithm, which will be programmed in chapter 7.

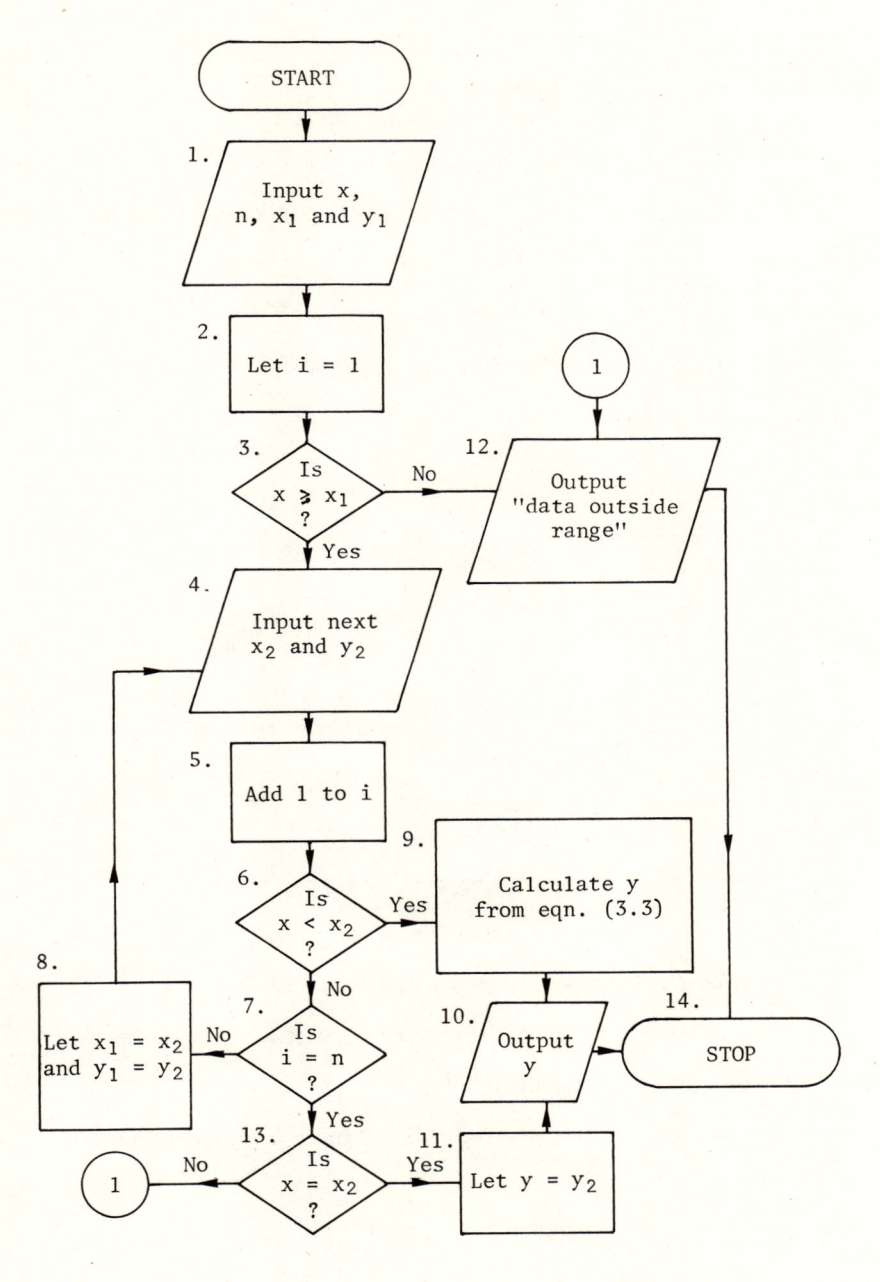

Figure 3.7 Flow chart for Mk. 2 linear interpolation algorithm

```
NEW OR OLD?
← NEW LINTERPMK2
← 100 REM LINEAR INTERPOLATION, MK.2
← 110 PRINT "TYPE VALUE OF X AT WHICH Y IS REQD."
← 120 INPUT X
← 130 PRINT "TYPE NO. OF DATA PTS."
← 140 INPUT N
← 150 PRINT "TYPE COORDS. OF 1ST. DATA PT. IN FORM X,Y"
← 160 INPUT X1,Y1
← 170 LET I=1
← 180 IF X>=X1 THEN 220
← 200 PRINT "DATA OUTSIDE RANGE"
← 210 GO TO 420
← 220 PRINT "TYPE COORDS. OF NEXT DATA PT."
← 230 INPUT X2,Y2
← 240 LET I=I+1
← 250 IF X<X2 THEN 300
← 260 IF I=N THEN 320
← 270 LET X1=X2
← 280 LET Y1=Y2
← 290 GO TO 220
← 300 LET Y=Y1+(Y2-Y1)*(X-X1)/(X2-X1)
← 310 GO TO 410
← 320 IF X<>X2 THEN 200
← 400 LET Y=Y2
← 410 PRINT "Y = ",Y,"WHEN X = ",X
← 420 END

← RUN
            RUN PROCEEDING
TYPE VALUE OF X AT WHICH Y IS REQD.
← 2.5
TYPE NO. OF DATA PTS.
← 4
TYPE COORDS. OF 1ST. DATA PT. IN FORM X,Y
← 1,1
TYPE COORDS. OF NEXT DATA PT.
← 2,4
TYPE COORDS. OF NEXT DATA PT.
← 3,7
Y =            5.5            WHEN X =         2.5
                  FINISHED
```

Figure 5.1 Program for Mk. 2 linear interpolation algorithm

5.4 CHECK YOUR PROGRESS

To check the understanding of the material in section 5.2 and its subsections, try the following exercises.

(1) Trace the following section of a BASIC program and decide what the output would be.

```
200 LET I=1
210 LET S=0
220 LET S=S+I*I
230 LET I=I+1
240 IF I<=4 THEN 220
250 PRINT S
```

(2) Translate into BASIC the following section of an algorithm.

(i) If a > b let b = a; if a ≤ b let b = 0.
(ii) Output the value of b.

Answers

(1) The output would be

30

being 1 + 4 + 9 + 16.

(2) The important lesson to be learnt here is that only one IF statement is required, thus

```
200 IF A>B THEN 230
210 LET B=0
220 GO TO 240
230 LET B=A
240 PRINT B
```

because, if A > B is false, that is, A < = B, then execution *automatically* continues at the statement following the IF.

5.5 A SECOND CASE STUDY - GRAPH-PLOTTING ON A TERMINAL

For our second case study in this chapter we are going to write a program to plot a graph on a terminal. The graph will be a simple parabola, representing the path of a projectile, but the concept can be applied to more complicated functions.

We shall use this example to illustrate three things: the use of branching statements to control loops, the control of PRINT statements to give the greatest possible flexibility of output format, and the use of standard BASIC functions.

If a projectile is projected from the origin of an X-Y coordinate system at an angle α with the positive X-axis and with an initial velocity V then the path of the projectile is the parabola

$$y = x \tan \alpha - gx^2 \sec^2 \alpha / 2V^2 \qquad (5.1)$$

We shall use the value 9.81 m s^{-2} for g.

The nearest we can get on a terminal to a continuous graph of this function is to print an X (or other suitable character) on successive lines, each line representing a value of x and the position on each line (that is, across the page) representing the

corresponding value of y. To ensure that the picture fits on to
the paper and that it is not too spread out, we need to assess the
maximum values of x and y that will be encountered. For our problem that is easy: the projectile lands on the (assumed flat) ground
when $y = 0$, that is, $x = V^2 \sin 2\alpha/g$, and its maximum height occurs
at the centre of the trajectory when $x = V^2 \sin 2\alpha/2g$, that is,
$y = V^2 \sin^2 \alpha/2g$. Let us assume a maximum initial velocity of
70 m s^{-1}, then the maximum values of x and y are approximately
500 m and 250 m.

Although each line can usually accommodate seventy-five characters we shall let each position represent a step of 4 m in y, so
that we reach about the sixty-fifth position for the maximum value
of y. To make the plot area approximately square we shall use a
maximum of about fifty lines for x, by letting each line represent
a step of 10 m in x.

An outline of the program is as follows.
(1) Print a scaled axis (horizontal) for y.
(2) For each $x = 0, 10, 20, 30, \ldots$ until $y < 0$, print the value of
x and then an X in the position corresponding to the value of
y.

(2) is just a loop controlled by adding 10 to x on each circuit
until the projectile lands. There is just one problem to be solved
before we introduce the BASIC necessary to write the program: how
do we find the number of the column corresponding to the value of y?
Since stepping from one column to the next is equivalent to an increase of 4 in y we need to be able to find the nearest multiple of
4 to the value of y; that multiple will give us the number of the
column in which the X is to be printed, and is given by the sequence
of calculations

(1) add 2 to y
(2) divide the result by 4
(3) take the integral part of the result, that is, chop off all the
decimal places.

This means, for example, that all the numbers in the interval
$10 \leq y < 14$ are associated with 12 and hence with column 3. (If
we did not add 2 then column 3 would represent $12 \leq y < 16$.)

Having sorted out the mathematics we can discuss the BASIC requirements for achieving the graphical output.

5.6   OUTPUT FORMATS

5.6.1 Horizontal control

In BASIC each line of seventy-five positions is divided into five
zones of fifteen positions each, and each zone into five sections
of three positions each. To begin printing at a particular place
on a line there are three devices that can be used: the items to
be printed can be separated by commas, or by semicolons, or the
print position can be specified explicitly using the TAB function.

The rules for the separators are as follows.

(1) If two items in a PRINT statement are separated by a comma then printing of the second item starts at the beginning of the next free zone (that is, position 1, 16, 31, 46 or 61).
(2) If two items in a PRINT statement are separated by a semicolon then printing of the second item starts at the beginning of the next free section if the first item is a number; if the first item is a string then printing of the second item starts immediately after the last character of the string.

The TAB function has the form

   TAB(X)

where X is any arithmetic expression. X is converted into an integer between 0 and 74 by first finding the remainder after division by 75 and then discarding the decimal places. If the result is less than or equal to the current output position the TAB has no effect; if it is greater then the next output operation starts at the indicated position if the TAB is followed by a semicolon, or at the beginning of the next zone after the indicated position if it is followed by a comma.

Figure 5.2 shows a program consisting almost entirely of PRINT statements, and the output from it, which demonstrates the possibilities described above.

The first four lines illustrate both the use of strings to give explanatory output and the way in which commas, and strings containing spaces, can be used to spread output across the page. For example, line 120 'prints' a space at column 1, another space at column 16 (the start of the next print zone), and prints OUTPUT starting at column 31 (the start of the third print zone). Lines 140 to 190 show the difference between the comma and semicolon as separators. Note that a column is allowed for the sign of a number. When the number is just two characters (for example, -2) the semicolon causes printing of the next item to start at the beginning of the next section, leaving just one space. When the number printed has three characters (for example, -12) the next output is due to start at the beginning of the next section; the semicolon then moves it to the beginning of the next section again - leaving three spaces (a completely blank section) between numbers. It should be clear from this that the use of the semicolon to separate the printing of purely numeric information may lead to jumbled and rather unreadable output.

Lines 180 and 190 demonstrate the effect of the comma and semicolon used after the TAB function. SEMICOLON starts at column 36, that is, its output starts immediately after TAB(35); COMMA starts at column 46, that is, the beginning of the next zone after column 35. Line 200 shows that TAB(10) has no effect when the output position is already beyond column 10. Lines 210 to 240 produce a parabolic graph and provide a preview of what we require for our projectile-plotting program. For each value of $X = 0(1)6$ an * is printed in column number INT(18*X-3*X*X), [INT(...) means take the

```
NEW OR OLD?
← NEW DEMO
← 100 PRINT "DEMO."
← 110 PRINT " ","OF"
← 120 PRINT " "," ","OUTPUT"
← 130 PRINT " "," "," ","FORMATS"
← 140 PRINT 1,2,3,4
← 150 PRINT 1;2;3;4
← 160 PRINT -1;-2;-3;-4
← 170 PRINT -11;-12;-13;
← 180 PRINT TAB(35),"COMMA"
← 190 PRINT TAB(35);"SEMICOLON"
← 200 PRINT "X";TAB(10);"Y";TAB(10);"Z"
← 210 LET X=0
← 220 PPINT TAB(18*X-3*X*X);"*"
← 230 LET X=X+1
← 240 IF X<7 THEN 220
← 250 END

← RUN
                    RUN PROCEEDING
DEMO.
               OF
                                    OUTPUT
                                                    FORMATS
 1                   2                 3              4
 1   2   3   4
-1  -2  -3  -4
-11     -12     -13


                                              COMMA
                                   SEMICOLON
X           YZ
*
             *
                          *
                              *
                          *
             *
*
                    FINISHED
```

Figure 5.2 Program illustrating output formats

nearest integer value less than or equal to the quantity in brackets
- see section 5.7] - so the distance across the page corresponds to
the value of the function $18X - 3X^2$. Each output line corresponds
to an X value; the first line to X = 0, the second line to X = 1,
and so on.

5.6.2 Vertical control

The vertical spacing of output is dictated by the following rules.

(1) If a PRINT statement ends with a comma or semicolon the next
    output continues on the same line. The effect of the comma or
    semicolon is as explained in the previous section.

(2) If a PRINT statement does not end in a comma or semicolon the next output will be at the beginning of the next line.

One consequence of (2) is that

    PRINT

by itself causes a blank line (unless the previous print statement ended with a comma or semicolon). For example

    100 PRINT
    110 PRINT "TABLE OF STRESS FACTORS"
    120 PRINT

causes a line space above and below the heading TABLE OF STRESS FACTORS when the program is run.

An example of the use of (1) is at the input of data

    100 PRINT "INPUT INITIAL VELOCITY";
    110 INPUT V

causes the output

    INPUT INITIAL VELOCITY ←

allowing the user to type the value of V on the same line, whereas omitting the semicolon at the end of line 100 would cause

    INPUT INITIAL VELOCITY
    ←

to appear.

5.7 STANDARD FUNCTIONS

The TAB function described in section 5.6.1 is a BASIC function automatically provided by the BASIC software stored in the computer. TAB can only be used in a PRINT statement. The other standard functions are listed below and can be used in any arithmetic expression in a BASIC program.

Function	Effect
SQR(X)	$\sqrt{X}$
ABS(X)	$\|X\|$
SIN(X)	sin X (X in radians)
COS(X)	cos X (X in radians)
ATN(X)	$\tan^{-1} X$ (answer in radians)
EXP(X)	e^X
LOG(X)	$\log_e X$
INT(X)	largest integer $\leq$ X (i.e. rounded down)
SGN(X)	sign of X i.e. -1 if X < 0
	0 if X = 0
	+1 if X > 0
RND(X)	pseudo-random number in the range 0 to 1

In each case X can be any arithmetic expression.

Hence the assignment statement corresponding to equation 5.1 (repeated here)

$$y = x \tan \alpha - gx^2 \sec^2 \alpha / 2V^2$$

might appear in BASIC as

LET Y=X*SIN(A)/COS(A)-G*X*X/(2*V*V*COS(A)*COS(A))

where A stands for α. In practice we shall precompute

S=X/(V*COS(A))

so that the assignment statement becomes

LET Y=V*S*SIN(A)-G*S*S/2

This is slightly more efficient and certainly less cumbersome than the version in one line given above.

We shall be using most of the other standard functions somewhere in this book. If it is unclear why they are needed, consider how one would otherwise instruct the computer to calculate, say, the cosine of a given angle - 'Go and look it up in some tables' is not very useful!

5.8 A PROGRAM FOR THE GRAPH-PLOTTING CASE STUDY

We are now in a position to retrace section 5.5 and translate our analysis of the graph-plotting problem into a BASIC program. We did not give a flow chart in section 5.5 because our knowledge of the possibilities in BASIC affects the way in which we solve the problem. A suitable flow chart is given in figure 5.3; most benefit will be obtained from studying it if section 5.5 is first re-read. Note that to leave room for the printed value of X at the beginning of each line we have arranged for y = 0 to correspond to position 6 by adding 6 to the expression that is supplied to the TAB function.

The corresponding program and output for the data V = 60 m s^{-1} and $\alpha = 75°$ are shown in figure 5.4. Pay particular attention to the way the loop that plots the graph is set up and controlled: X is 'initialised' to zero before the loop starts, at each pass through the loop it is incremented by 10, and the loop is broken when y < 0.

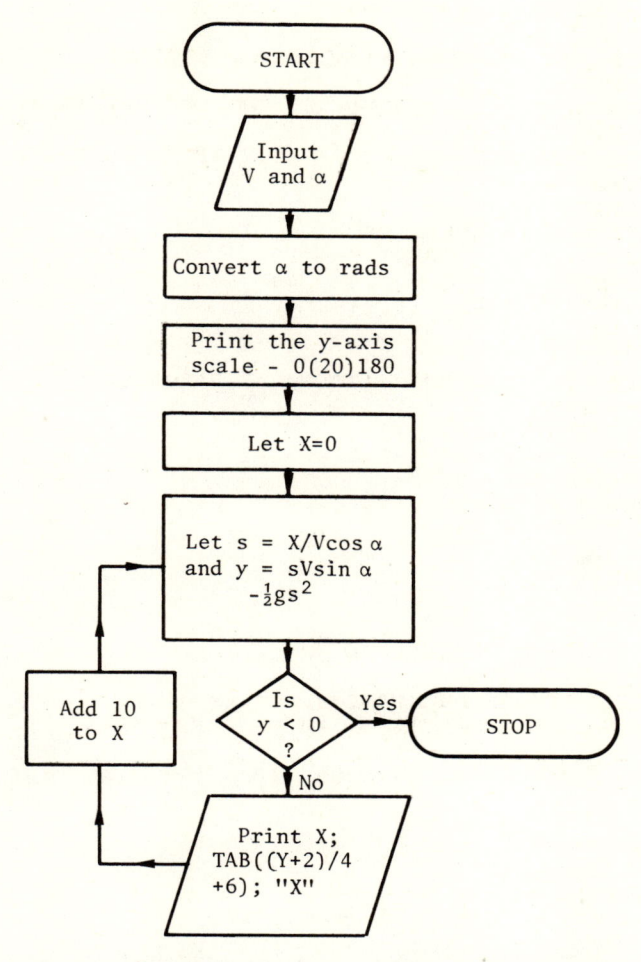

```
                    ┌─────────┐
                    │  START  │
                    └────┬────┘
                         │
                    ╱─────────╲
                   ╱   Input   ╲
                   ╲  V and α  ╱
                    ╲─────────╱
                         │
                 ┌───────────────┐
                 │ Convert α to rads │
                 └───────┬───────┘
                         │
                 ┌───────────────┐
                 │ Print the y-axis │
                 │ scale - 0(20)180 │
                 └───────┬───────┘
                         │
                 ┌───────────────┐
                 │   Let X=0     │
                 └───────┬───────┘
                         │
                 ┌───────────────┐
         ┌──────→│ Let s = X/Vcosα │
         │       │ and y = sVsinα  │
         │       │   -½gs²         │
         │       └───────┬───────┘
         │               │
   ┌─────────┐       ╱───────╲        ┌────────┐
   │ Add 10  │      ╱   Is    ╲ Yes   │        │
   │  to X   │←────╲  y < 0   ╱──────→│  STOP  │
   └─────────┘      ╲    ?   ╱        └────────┘
         ↑           ╲──┬──╱
         │              │ No
         │       ╱─────────────╲
         │      ╱   Print X;     ╲
         └─────╲ TAB((Y+2)/4     ╱
                ╲ +6); "X"      ╱
                 ╲─────────────╱
```

Figure 5.3 Flow chart for graph plotting problem

```
NEW OR OLD?
← NEW GRAPH
← 100 REM              GRAPH PLOTTING PROGRAM
← 110 PRINT
← 120 PRINT "INPUT VELOCITY OF PROJECTION, IN M/S";
← 130 INPUT V
← 140 PRINT "INPUT ANGLE OF PROJECTION, IN DEGREES";
← 150 INPUT A
← 160 PRINT
← 170 LET A=3.14159*A/180
← 180 REM              PRINT Y-AXIS
← 190 PRINT "    Y 0     20    40    60    80    100   120";
← 191 PRINT "  140   160   180"
← 200 PRINT
← 210 PRINT " X"
← 220 REM              PRINT GRAPH OF PARABOLA
← 230 LET X=0
← 240 LET S=X/(V*COS(A))
← 250 LET Y=S*V*SIN(A)-9.81*S*S/2
← 260 IF Y<0 THEN 300
← 270 PRINT X; TAB((Y+2)/4+6);"X"
← 280 LET X=X+10
← 290 GO TO 240
← 300 END

← RUN
              RUN PROCEEDING

INPUT VELOCITY OF PROJECTION, IN M/S← 60
INPUT ANGLE OF PROJECTION, IN DEGREES← 75

      Y 0    20    40    60    80   100   120   140   160   180

 X
  0     X
 10          X
 20               X
 30                 X
 40                      X
 50                          X
 60                             X
 70                              X
 80                                 X
 90                                   X
100                                  X
110                                 X
120                              X
130                           X
140                       X
150                  X
160              X
170         X
180     X

                    FINISHED
         Figure 5.4  Program for graph plotting problem
```

5.9 POSTSCRIPT

In this chapter our main innovation is the capability of branching in a BASIC program using the GO TO and IF statements. In general these allow logical decisions to be made by the computer on the basis of the information stored in it, and in particular they allow the construction of loops in programs.

In our first case study the loop was designed to test successive intervals to find the one within which a given number lay. In the second case study the loop printed out the positions on a graph of the values of the expression on the right of equation 5.1, for successive values of x. As further new material this second example introduced output formatting and standard functions. All of these ideas will be used continuously in the remainder of the book.

EXERCISES

5.1. Improve the simultaneous-equations program of exercise 4.5 by protecting it against the possibility of instability described in section 3.2 (that is, stop the program if $|a_{11}a_{22} - a_{12}a_{21}| < e$, where e is a tolerance to be input as data, and print a warning message "NO SOLUTION").

5.2 Write BASIC programs for the flow charts of exercises 3.1, 3.3 and 3.4.

5.3 Draw a flow chart and write a BASIC program to do the calculations involved in a simple weight analysis. Assume that the object being analysed is made of one material so that we only need to calculate the volume, and assume that the volume is approximated by a set of rectangular and circular cylinders. Each pass through the program requires the input of a code number (say +1 = rectangular cylinder, -1 = circular cylinder, 0 = no more data) and the dimensions of the corresponding cylinder. The output will be just the total volume.

5.4 Write a BASIC program to convert Cartesian coordinates to polar coordinates; the formulae are

$$r = \sqrt{(x^2 + y^2)}$$

$$\theta = \begin{cases} \tan^{-1}(y/x) & \text{if } x > 0 \\ \tan^{-1}(y/x) + 180° & \text{if } x < 0, y > 0 \\ \tan^{-1}(y/x) - 180° & \text{if } x < 0, y < 0 \\ 0° & \text{if } x = y = 0 \\ 90° & \text{if } x = 0, y > 0 \\ -90° & \text{if } x = 0, y < 0 \end{cases}$$

Arrange for the program to take a sequence of (x, y) pairs, to be terminated when $x > 10^9$, and output x, y, r and θ in each case in a table with headings, as follows.

```
    x    y    r    deg.
    3   -4    5   -53.13
    etc
```

(Hint: try to use the SGN function - see section 5.7.)

6 PROGRAMMING PRACTICE

6.1 INTRODUCTION

We can now write simple but useful BASIC programs. Before we go on to more sophisticated BASIC statements, we must consider some practical aspects of programming.

This chapter exists mostly because the programs we write are almost never perfect; in fact it is impossible to say what perfection means in relation to computer programs. In the simplest case we just make mistakes, and we make them quite often, so we first discuss common mistakes, particularly those made by beginning programmers. Then we describe how to change BASIC programs, whether to correct mistakes or to add new statements. Some program faults only show themselves in certain circumstances, for example, if certain data are input; it is therefore important that we check comprehensively that our programs work as they are intended, so we have included a section on program-testing. Finally, if a program is to be useful in the future, whether to the writer or to some other user, and if it is to be fairly easy to make changes, then it is necessary that we write a description of how to use the program. So the final section of this chapter is a brief account of how a program might be documented.

6.2 TYPICAL MISTAKES

If this book is read while doing a practical course in BASIC, the most common mistake of the new programmer will have been discovered - the assumption that the computer is 'kindhearted' and will not mind if BASIC statements are not exactly as they should be.

Here are some statements that have appeared in programs written by students.

```
100 IF A EQUALS 0 THEN 210
200 OUTPUT X
300 IF |X|<1E-6 THEN 370
400 READ A=3,B=5,C=9
500 DATA A=3,B=5,C=9
600 LET X=0 AND Y=0
```

The mistakes in these statements should be apparent; correcting them has been set as an exercise at the end of the chapter. The point to be emphasised is that the form of BASIC statements is quite strict, so get used to checking them against the relevant format. (We have provided a summary on the cover of this book.)

The other common mistake by the beginner, apart from the involuntary ones such as missing out statements, is to not follow the logic of the algorithm correctly (assuming that the algorithm is correct!). A typical example is the omission of a GO TO statement from the program when there is an unconditional branch in the flow chart. This mistake usually occurs because the branch is not indicated by a box in the flow chart. It is impossible to catalogue such mistakes; we can only emphasise that the program will be of little value if it does not represent the algorithm correctly and that it is essential to check that the program and the flow chart agree.

If the algorithm is being developed by programming it, then mistakes may, of course, occur in the algorithm. In this case it is most important when correcting mistakes to alter the flow chart as well as the program. We shall return to this in section 6.5.

As more experience is gained in programming, the mistakes made are more likely to be ones such as inserting a new corrected statement into a program and forgetting to delete the old incorrect statement. As in all things, good results need careful preparation and thorough workmanship.

6.3 EDITING PROGRAMS

When working off-line, with the program on punched cards or paper tape, correction of a program is usually a matter of punching new cards or pieces of paper tape and replacing the incorrect statements. The program can then be rerun.

When working on-line at a terminal, it is clearly undesirable to have to retype the whole program in order to correct perhaps one mistake. Accordingly, all BASIC systems allow statements to be changed or inserted at any invitation to type (except when the invitation is to supply data during a run of the program), by simply typing the statements, with their line numbers, in the normal way. Indeed this is the whole point of numbering every statement; regardless of the physical order in which you enter statements the BASIC system will process them in the order of their line numbers.

As an example suppose we are typing into the computer the triangle area program of figure 4.4 and suppose that, without noticing, we type

    120   INPUT A,B

instead of

    120   INPUT A,B,C

and that we omit to type statement 140, then the following sequence will occur

    ← RUN
                   RUN PROCEEDING
   INPUT LENGTHS OF SIDES
   ← 3,4,5
             TOO MANY
             INPUT 2
   ←

At this point you cannot retype line 120 correctly because the computer is demanding data. The simplest way to deal with this is to give two numbers and then break into the program (or let it finish if it is as short as the triangle area program). At the subsequent invitation to type you can then correct line 120, and rerun the program as follows.

```
   120 INPUT A,B,C
 ← RUN
                    RUN PROCEEDING
   INPUT LENGTHS OF SIDES
 ← 3,4,5
   WHAT UNITS OF LENGTH ARE YOU USING?
   AREA OF TRIANGLE WITH SIDES OF LENGTH
       3              4              5
       IS             6              SQUARE

                    FINISHED
 ←
```

At this point we notice that we had no invitation to type the units of length - the output is correspondingly confused - and that line 140 is missing, so we simply type

```
   140 INPUT L£
 ← RUN
```

and this time the results will be as shown in figure 4.4.

It is of course possible that when a program fails to work as expected the cause of the failure is not clear. In this case it is sensible to leave the terminal and to investigate the problem at leisure, rather than take up terminal time that someone else might be able to use. It is also tempting to guess at the cause of the failure and, possibly, make things worse by incorrectly amending the program.

It is not reasonable to have to retype the program when returning to the terminal with the mistakes corrected, so most BASIC systems have a facility for storing programs in the backing store of the computer, from where they can be recalled when needed.

The BASIC command that achieves this storage is

SAVE

When typing this command, the version of the program that is saved is the one that is currently in the working area of the computer store, that is, complete with any amendments made since it was first entered. The program is saved with whatever name it was given in the NEW command (or OLD command - see below).

To retrieve the program at a later time the OLD command is used; it has the same form as the NEW command, that is

OLD program name

To erase a stored program from the backing store the UNSAVE command is used; it has the form

UNSAVE program name

Here is a typical sequence of events that could occur in entering and correcting a BASIC program.

First attempt

```
NEW OR OLD?
← NEW PROG
...
...   (program typed into the computer)
...
← RUN
...
...   (data entered and results printed)
...
← SAVE
← BYE
```

Second attempt

```
NEW OR OLD?
← OLD PROG
...
...   (new and/or amended statements)
...
← RUN
...
...   (data entered and results printed)
...
← UNSAVE PROG
← SAVE
← BYE
```

Note how the pair of commands

UNSAVE PROG
SAVE

deletes the old version of PROG from the backing store and stores the new version in its place (with the same name - PROG in this case).

If the process of editing and restoring is carried out more than twice, it may be desirable to make a copy of the latest version of the program before considering further changes, or simply for documentation purposes. This can be achieved by the command

LIST

There are ways of making this command list certain lines only, but we shall not give any details here. Later in the book (section 9.3) we shall briefly consider commands for renaming a program and for deleting lines from a program. A statement can always be deleted by typing just its line number; this replaces the statement by a blank statement.

Finally, two points to note about editing. Firstly, all the above can be done equally well off-line, with cards or paper tape, but with the obvious disadvantage of the longer time lag between changes and their effects when compared with the almost immediate response of a terminal. Secondly, it will be found that numbering the statements in the original program in steps of 10 is usually necessary because it quite often happens that say, five or six extra statements need to be inserted between two original statements - for example, to print out some extra information.

6.4 PROGRAM-TESTING

It is not sufficient to write a program to solve a particular problem and run it with the data for that problem, unless there is a very good independent check on the validity of the results. It is far better, if time allows, to design an algorithm that solves a class of problems and to test the program with a series of simple problems from that class that are carefully designed to check each aspect of the program.

We have already given an example of this in connection with the Mark 2 version of our linear interpolation algorithm. This interpolates for the value of y corresponding to a given x when the data (x_1, y_1), (x_2, y_2), ..., (x_n, y_n) are known, where $x_1 < x_2 < ... < x_n$. The algorithm is designed to reject values of x that satisfy $x < x_1$ or $x > x_n$, and the case when $x = x_n$ has to be dealt with separately. Hence to test the program fully we decided on a simple set of data: (1, 1), (2, 4), (3, 7) and (4, 10), and we suggested that interpolation should be attempted at x = 2.5 (straightforward, we should get y = 5.5), x = 4 (tests special case of $x = x_n$, we should get y = 10), x = 0 and x = 5 (tests rejection due to $x < x_1$ and $x > x_n$).

The overriding principle for tests like these is that they should be simple, but comprehensive. We shall describe tests for some other programs later in the book.

6.5 DOCUMENTATION

Professional programmers spend much of their time documenting the progress of their work and writing guides for the users of their programs. In the following we describe, briefly, how these two aspects of documentation can be achieved in a modest fashion.

6.5.1 Documenting program development

Once the specification for the program is decided (and that may be sufficiently complicated to need documenting too), the first flow chart has been constructed and a program written, then the development stage begins. During development it is very easy to lose track of the latest version of the program and to forget why certain changes were made. Therefore it is advisable to keep a record of each attempt to run the program, with the following information

(1) date and time (if more than one run per day)
(2) copy of program used and corresponding flow chart
(3) data used, that is, which test problem
(4) results
(5) brief description of reasons for any amendments
(6) list of amendments you intend to make to flow chart and/or program.

To this file of information can be added a copy of the process of amending the program if done at a terminal.

Items (1), (3), (5) and (6) can be written on the print-out (from the terminal or line printer), which contains a copy of the program and the results of the run.

Note that implicit in the above is the recommendation that if the mistake being corrected is a mistake in the algorithm then the flow chart should be corrected first, and then the program. At all times the latest version of the program should correspond to the latest version of the flow chart.

6.5.2 Documenting a finished program

When the program is satisfactory then the final entry in the development file will contain the finished program and flow chart. To complete the documentation, so that anyone could use the program in the future without any great difficulty, the following should be described.

(1) A suitable set of test problems with expected output (if not already documented); these will be needed if the program is subsequently changed for any reason.
(2) How the input data are to be prepared and entered.
(3) How the output should be interpreted (if it is not obvious).
(4) A typical run of the program, showing the program retrieved using the OLD command, showing it RUN, the data entered and the results produced.

Anyone wishing to use the program would be given copies of (2), (3) and (4).

Here are examples of (2) and (3) for the Mark 2 linear interpolation program (figure 5.1).

INPUT The data required by the program are

(1) the value of x at which y is required (X)
(2) the number of data points (N)
(3) the coordinates of each data point in the form x, y (one point at a time).

In each case the program will clearly specify the next data required.

OUTPUT The output will be the estimated value of y for the given value of x, unless x is not in the interval $x_1 \leq x \leq x_n$ in which case a warning message "DATA OUTSIDE RANGE" will be printed.

In later chapters of this book we shall sometimes document the input requirements and the output obtainable for a program, as further examples of the form exemplified above. However, it should be noted that when working interactively with BASIC the need for such documentation can be minimised by proper use of the PRINT statement. This is demonstrated by the output from and input to the program of figure 5.1, where data requests and results are fully explained as the program runs.

Finally a disclaimer: this section does not pretend to be a full description of how a professional computer programmer documents his work. The main reason for including the section is to emphasise that documentation of work is at least advisable, and probably essential. The details are simply suggestions based on experience of writing computer programs to solve problems for scientists and engineers.

EXERCISES

6.1 Correct the BASIC statements given in section 6.2.
6.2 (a) Devise a set of test data, and
(b) write an input/output documentation for the quadratic-equation-solving program resulting from exercises 3.1 and 5.2.

7 BASIC-ARRAYS

7.1 CASE STUDY - LINEAR INTERPOLATION MARK 3

For the first half of this chapter we shall be concerned with writing a BASIC program for the flow chart of figure 3.9. It may be helpful for reading this chapter if chapter 3 is quickly read through again, from section 3.3 onwards; at the very least section 3.6 should be reread, checking that it is clear how figure 3.9 solves the linear-interpolation problem as set there. (Figure 3.9 is repeated in section 7.5 for easy reference while reading this chapter.)

The main difference between the Mark 2 and Mark 3 algorithms is that the Mark 3 version can cope with m interpolations (that is, any given number), whereas the Mark 2 version can only interpolate once. To be able to do this the Mark 3 version requires the input and storage of *all* the data points, whereas the Mark 2 version inputs and discards them one at a time in such a way that only two adjacent points are stored at any instant. This storage of all the data points requires the concept of an *array* of numbers. In fact we need two arrays: the array of x-coordinates $(x_1, x_2, \ldots, x_n)$ and the array of corresponding y-coordinates $(y_1, y_2, \ldots, y_n)$. For example, the test data we used for the Mark 2 version consisted of the data points (1, 1), (2, 4), (3, 7) and (4, 10). In this case n = 4 and the two arrays would be (1, 2, 3, 4) and (1, 4, 7, 10).

In computing terminology these one-dimensional arrays are sometimes called *lists*; in mathematics they are called *vectors*. In the second case study of this chapter we shall encounter *two*-dimensional arrays, called *tables* in computing, and *matrices* in mathematics. So our first need in this chapter is to be able to store numbers in arrays in BASIC. One-dimensional arrays are dealt with in section 7.2 and two-dimensional arrays in section 7.7.

There is another new feature in figure 3.9: the loops are desscribed differently. For example, to input the coordinates (x_1, y_1), $(x_2, y_2), \ldots, (x_n, y_n)$, instead of the process

(1) Let i = 1
(2) Input x_i and y_i
(3) If i = n go to 5
(4) Otherwise add 1 to i and go back to 2
(5) ...
etc.

we have simply

(1) Input x_i and y_i for i = 1(1)n (i.e. for i taking all values from 1 to n in steps of 1)
etc.

Apart from simplifying the flow chart this representation for a loop leads us to a correspondingly simple pair of BASIC statements, which allow us very easily to set up loops in a BASIC program. These statements are described in section 7.3.

7.2 ONE-DIMENSIONAL ARRAYS IN BASIC

It is quite natural for us to write the n x-coordinates as x_1, x_2, ..., x_n rather than, say, a, b, c, ..., q, because each coordinate is one of a set of numbers all playing a similar part in the problem, so it is reasonable that they all have the same 'name' (x). The subscripts 1, 2, ..., n allow us to distinguish between the n numbers *and* tell us that there are precisely n of them.

Not surprisingly BASIC allows us a similar facility. Instead of x_1, x_2, ..., x_n we write X(1), X(2), ..., X(N). The array variable name (X in this case) can often only be a letter, but some BASIC systems allow a letter followed by a digit as for the names of ordinary numeric variables. The quantity in parentheses, called the subscript, can be any arithmetic expression, but only makes sense as a positive integer - although, once again, BASIC systems do vary, and a zero subscript is sometimes allowed. Non-integer subscripts are truncated, so A(2.3) is interpreted as A(2), and H(2*E+1), where E = 1.9, is interpreted as H(4). Normally, however, the subscript is either a positive integer constant, for example Q(25), or a variable taking positive integer values, for example Z(K), where K = 1, 2, 3, ...

For our case study we need the two arrays X(I) and Y(I), where I = 1, 2, ..., N. In most BASIC systems we can simply use these subscripted variables provided I does not exceed 10 (that is, provided we have not more than ten data points in our particular problem). If more than ten elements are needed in a list then we have to inform the computer through a DIM statement. (DIM stands for dimension.) It has the format

    DIM arrayname1 (sub1), arrayname2 (sub2), etc.

where sub1 is at least as big as the largest subscript that arrayname1 requires, and similarly sub2 for arrayname2, and so on. The last entry in the DIM statement is *not* followed by a comma. For example, suppose we are to have a maximum of twenty data points in our interpolation problem, then we need the statement

    DIM X(20),Y(20)

Having thus asked the computer for room to store twenty x- and twenty y-coordinates it is *not* necessary to use all of that storage. If in a particular case N = 12 then the remaining eight locations in each list are simply ignored. However, since statements are very easily changed in BASIC, it is quite usual for the DIM statements to state precisely the storage required.

7.3 FOR LOOPS

In the introductory section 7.1 we described the essential difference between our previous approach to controlling loops and the neater, more elegant approach that we are about to adopt.

   Here is a translation into BASIC of the first process given there.

```
200 LET I=1
210 READ X(I),Y(I)
220 IF I=N THEN 250
230 LET I=I+1
240 GO TO 210
250 ...
```

The second process was just one line, but needs slightly more in BASIC

```
200 FOR I=1 TO N STEP 1
210 READ X(I),Y(I)
220 NEXT I
```

The innovations here are, of course, the FOR and NEXT statements. Note how close the format of the FOR statement is to the corresponding 'for i = 1(1)n' of the flow chart. In general the format is

   FOR variable=expr1 TO expr2 STEP expr3

where variable means a numeric variable name, and expr1, expr2 and expr3 are arithmetic expressions. The NEXT statement has the format

   NEXT variable

where variable is the same variable name as in the corresponding FOR statement.

   Here are some more examples.

```
FOR J=K TO 20 STEP 2
...
...
NEXT J
FOR X=0 TO 1 STEP 0.1
...
...
NEXT X
FOR P=Z*2 TO -Z*2 STEP -2
...
...
NEXT P
```

In each case the statements between the FOR and the NEXT are executed as many times as are indicated by the FOR statement. In the first example above, if K = 6, say, then the loop is traversed eight times with J taking the successive values 6, 8, 10, 12, 14, 16, 18 and 20. In the second example the loop is executed eleven times with X taking the values 0, 0.1, 0.2, ..., 0.9 and 1.0.

The only allowable deviation from the given format of the FOR statement occurs where the increment (expr3) has the constant value 1. In this case the STEP part can be omitted. Hence, for our case study, we can write

```
FOR I=1 TO N
READ X(I),Y(I)
NEXT I
```

There are two other loops in our case study flow chart (figure 3.9). The outer one of the two causes the complete interpolation process to be carried out m times, and the inner one searches for the interval within which the current interpolation is to be made. (This is the part already achieved in the Mark 2 version of the algorithm.) When two or more loops interact in this way they must not cross one another but must be 'nested', so that any inner loop is entirely within any outer loop.

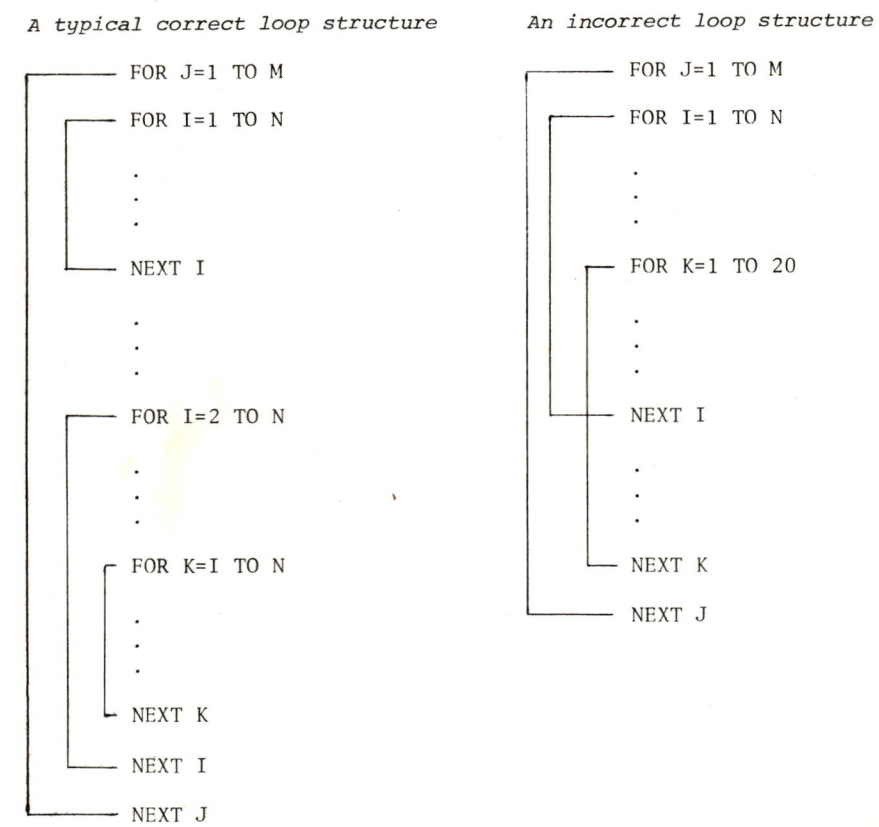

A typical correct loop structure   *An incorrect loop structure*

```
┌─── FOR J=1 TO M              ┌─── FOR J=1 TO M
│  ┌─ FOR I=1 TO N             │  ┌─ FOR I=1 TO N
│  │    .                      │  │    .
│  │    .                      │  │    .
│  │    .                      │  │    .
│  └─ NEXT I                   │  │  ┌─ FOR K=1 TO 20
│       .                      │  │  │    .
│       .                      │  │  │    .
│       .                      │  │  │    .
│  ┌─ FOR I=2 TO N             │  └─ NEXT I
│  │    .                      │     .
│  │    .                      │     .
│  │    .                      │     .
│  │  ┌─ FOR K=I TO N          │  └─ NEXT K
│  │  │   .                    └──── NEXT J
│  │  │   .
│  │  │   .
│  │  └─ NEXT K
│  └─── NEXT I
└────── NEXT J
```

This book aims to be introductory rather than comprehensive so we have deliberately not said what will happen in all possible cases when a FOR loop is used. Such knowledge can be obtained from BASIC manuals written for the computer system used, or by pestering experienced users, or by experiment. For example, what would happen if the following statement occurred in a program?

    FOR I=1 TO 5 STEP -1

In fact the statements between the FOR and corresponding NEXT would not be executed at all.

7.4 CHECK YOUR PROGRESS

These questions are designed to check the understanding of essential ideas in sections 7.2 and 7.3.

(1) For what values of K would the following loops be executed?

(a)   FOR K=2 TO 4
        ...
        NEXT K
(b)   FOR K=2 TO -4 STEP -2
        ...
        NEXT K
(c)   FOR K=-N TO 4*N STEP N
        ...
        NEXT K

(2) What would be the value of T at the end of the following section of program?

        300 LET T=0
        310 FOR I=1 TO 5
        320 READ X(I)
        330 LET T=T+X(I)
        340 NEXT I
        350 DATA -2,1,0,5,-1

(3) What is the mistake in the following?

        100 DIM A(15)
        110 READ N
        120 FOR I=1 TO N
        130 READ A(I)
        140 NEXT I
        150 DATA 20
        160 DATA ......

Answers

(1) (a) 2,3,4
(b) 2,0,-2,-4
(c) -N, 0, N, 2*N, 3*N, 4*N

(2) 3 i.e. -2 + 1 + 0 + 5 + (-1)

(3) N is given as 20 in the data statement, so lines 120-140, say, read A(1), ..., A(20), but the DIM statement only allows the existence of A(1), ..., A(15).

7.5 A PROGRAM FOR THE CASE STUDY

We now have sufficient material to code the flow chart of figure 3.9 (repeated here for your convenience); the resulting program is shown in figure 7.1. As usual we have made the input to and output from the program easy to understand by printing out suitable explanations. But in this example, for the first time in this book, we have used a DATA statement and a corresponding READ statement. The reason for this is that the data points (x_1, y_1), (x_2, y_2), ..., (x_n, y_n) may be sufficiently numerous for us to be wasting time at the terminal by typing them in point by point. Remember that DATA statements are accessed by READ statements in the order of their line numbers, the READ statements working through the DATA statements taking as many numbers as they need. After each READ operation a pointer is set at the next piece of data ready for the next READ operation. So, in the program given, the first READ operation allocates 1 to X(1) and 1 to Y(1), the next READ (when I = 2) allocates 2 to X(2) and 4 to Y(2), and so on.

To use this program for a different problem requires new DATA and DIM statements to be prepared. Here is a possible input/output documentation.

INPUT (1) Before running the program type in new DATA statement(s) containing the coordinates of the data points in the order $x_1, y_1, x_2, y_2, ..., x_n, y_n$. The line numbers of the data statements must start at 400 and can continue to 409.

(2) If you have more than twenty data points (the program is set up for a maximum of twenty) type in a new DIM statement of the form

110 DIM X(N),Y(N)

where N must be replaced by the actual number of data points.

(3) During execution of the program you will be asked to input

(a) the number of data points (N)
(b) the number of interpolations required (M)
(c) the successive x-coordinates of the points at which interpolation is required.

OUTPUT The output consists of a table of the given x-coordinates and the calculated y-coordinates. If any x value is outside the interval $x_1 \leq x \leq x_n$ a warning message "X OUTSIDE RANGE" is printed.

Before going on to our next case study here are some more comments on the program of figure 7.1.

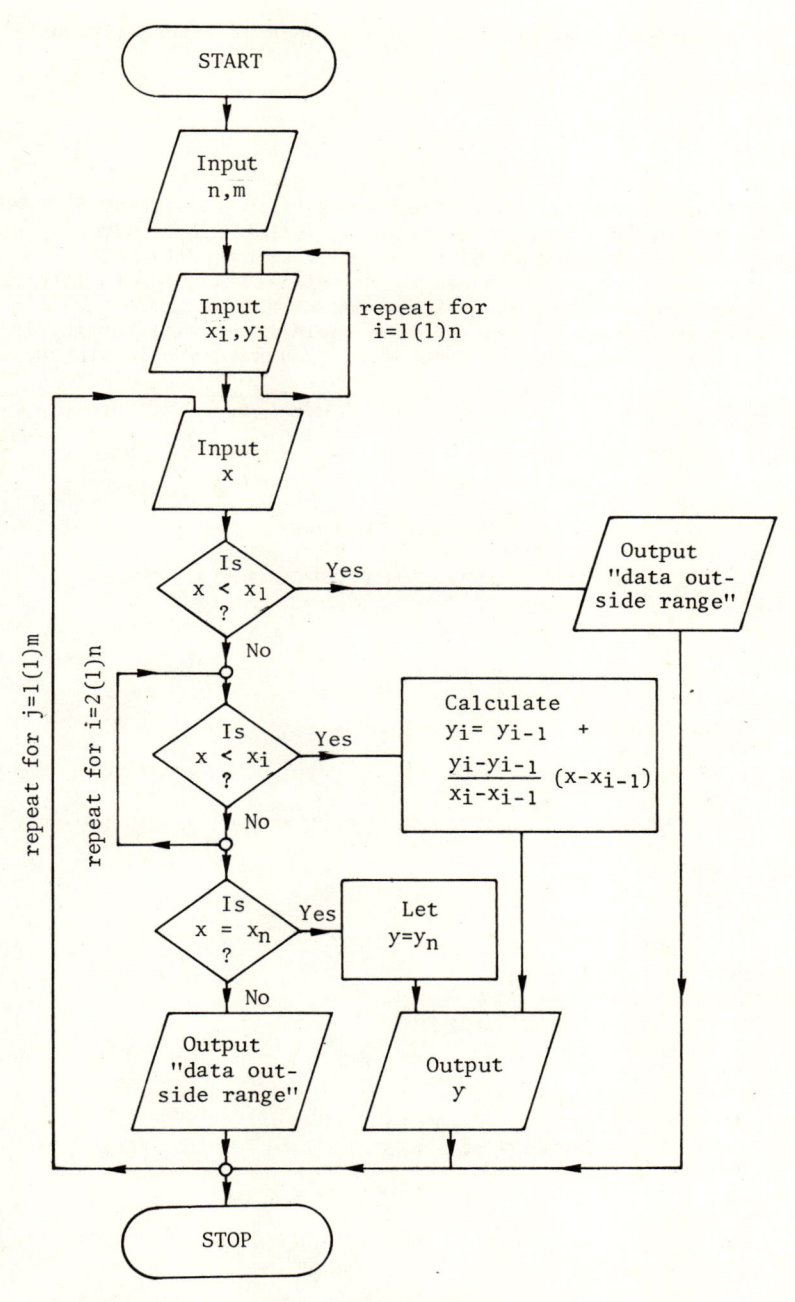

Figure 3.9 Flow chart for Mk. 3 linear interpolation algorithm

61

(1) In the outer loop controlling the number of interpolations

```
FOR J=1 TO M
...
...
NEXT J
```

J is not actually used but merely acts as a counting device. In the other loops the controlling variable I is actually used to reference elements of the X and Y arrays. In fact J is not necessary and it would be a perfectly reasonable alternative simply to branch back for more x values until the user has completed his work, when he would input some terminating number. This would be recognised by a suitable IF statement.

```
NEW OR OLD?
← OLD LINTERPMK3
← LIST

LINTERPMK3     ON 09/03/76 AT 18.29.59

100 REM                  LINEAR INTERPOLATION, MK.3
110 DIM X(20),Y(20)
120 PRINT "TYPE NO. OF DATA PTS.";
130 INPUT N
140 PRINT "TYPE NO. OF INTERPOLATIONS REQD.";
150 INPUT M
160 FOR I=1 TO N
170 READ X(I),Y(I)
180 NEXT I
190 PRINT
200 PRINT "AFTER 'X=' APPEARS TYPE NEXT VALUE OF X"
210 PRINT "AT WHICH Y IS REQD."
220 PRINT
230 PRINT " "," X"," Y"
240 FOR J=1 TO M
250 PRINT "X=";
260 INPUT X
270 IF X>=X(1) THEN 300
280 PRINT "X OUTSIDE RANGE"
290 GO TO 380
300 FOR I=2 TO N
310 IF X>=X(I) THEN 340
320 LET Z=(Y(I)-Y(I-1))/(X(I)-X(I-1))
321 LET Y=Y(I-1)+Z*(X-X(I-1))
330 GO TO 370
340 NEXT I
350 IF X<>X(N) THEN 280
360 LET Y=Y(N)
370 PRINT " ",X,Y
380 NEXT J
390 PRINT
400 DATA 1,1,2,4,3,7,4,10
410 END
```

```
← RUN
              RUN PROCEEDING
TYPE NO. OF DATA PTS.← 4
TYPE NO. OF INTERPOLATIONS REQD.← 4

AFTER 'X=' APPEARS TYPE NEXT VALUE OF X
AT WHICH Y IS REQD.

                     X                Y
X=← 2.5
                    2.5              5.5
X=← 0
X OUTSIDE RANGE
X=← 4
                     4                10
X=← 5
X OUTSIDE RANGE


              FINISHED
```

Figure 7.1 Program for Mk. 3 linear interpolation algorithm

For example, a number larger than one million could be used to indicate that the user has finished.

Statements 140, 150 and 240 would then not be needed; statement 380 would become

380 GO TO 250

and the new statement

265 IF X>1E6 THEN 390

would be inserted. (Remember: 1E6 means 1×10^6.) This use of a terminating element to indicate the end of a list of data is a very common device in computing. (See exercises 3.3 and 3.4.)

(2) Note how much work has gone into the layout and content of the output; this is extra to the work of constructing the flow chart.

(3) Look closely at the loop of statements 300 to 340. In the first place we have chosen to negate the proposition in the IF statement. If $x \geq x_i$ we wish to increase i and repeat the loop. To do this we jump to the *end* of the loop, *not* the beginning. If statement 310 were

IF X>=X(I) THEN 300

we would start again at I = 2 instead of continuing with the next I value. A similar situation occurs at statement 290.

7.6 A SECOND CASE STUDY - MATRIX MANIPULATION

Students of computer programming generally find the manipulation of two-dimensional arrays difficult. Consequently the problem we shall consider in this section will not be very interesting or profound in its own right but will be concerned just with manipulating a table of data. Before describing the problem we must discuss some necessary terminology.

A two-dimensional array of data is characterised by its number of rows and its number of columns. A table or matrix with M rows and N columns is said to be an M by N table or matrix. Here is a 2 by 4 matrix

$$\begin{pmatrix} -1 & 0 & 1 & 5 \\ 0 & 0 & 3 & -2 \end{pmatrix}$$

If we give a table the name A, say, then, just as the ith element of a list X is written X(I), so an element in the ith row and jth column of A is written A(I, J). For example, referring to the matrix above, A(1, 1) = -1 and A(2, 3) = 3.

Now here is the process we shall program in BASIC to illustrate the manipulation of tables.

(1) Input M and N
(2) Input the M by N matrix A
(3) Find the position in the matrix of the element of largest magnitude; let that element be A(K, L)
(4) Exchange the first and Kth rows of A
(5) Exchange the first and Lth columns of A
(6) Print out the transformed matrix A.

Although this process has no intrinsic value it is sometimes used within elimination methods for solving simultaneous linear equations. The process is usually called 'full pivoting'.

7.7 TWO-DIMENSIONAL ARRAYS IN BASIC

The rules for using tables in BASIC are simple extensions of those for lists. The array name is a single letter; the two subscripts are enclosed in parentheses after the name (as described in the last section) and follow the same rules as for single subscripts: tables with subscripts not greater than 10 need not appear in a DIM statement - hence a 10 by 10 array is the largest that does not need a DIM entry. Here is an example of a DIM statement containing a mixture of lists and tables.

    DIM A(20,20),X(2,20),C(15),D(20,5)

So A is to have at most 20 rows and 20 columns, X at most 2 rows and 20 columns, etc.

7.8 CHECK YOUR PROGRESS

These questions are designed to check the understanding of material in section 7.7, and the understanding of how two-dimensional arrays are set up and manipulated.

(1) What is the following section of program achieving: (a), (b) or (c)?

(a) Adding together all the elements of the M by N matrix A.
(b) Adding together all the elements of the Ith row of A.
(c) Adding together all the elements of the Jth column of A.

```
200 LET S=0
210 FOR J=1 TO N
220 LET S=S+A(I,J)
230 NEXT J
```

(2) Write a DIM statement for a program involving two 15 by 15 matrices, two vectors each with 15 elements, and a vector with 3 elements.

Answers

(1) (b) - note that I does not change in the program segment, so all the action is in the Ith row.

(2) DIM A(15,15),B(15,15),U(15),V(15),S(3) for example [S(3) could be omitted since the maximum subscript is less than 11.]

7.9 A PROGRAM FOR THE MATRIX MANIPULATION PROBLEM

We shall discuss the parts (2) to (6) of the process given in section 7.6, part (1) being the straightforward input of the array dimensions M and N.

(2) We can input a matrix row by row, or column by column; we shall choose the former method. So we shall want to input A(I,J) for each I and J, in the order: A(1,1), A(1,2), ..., A(1,N) (the first row), A(2,1), A(2,2), ..., A(2,N) (the second row), etc., until finally A(M,1), A(M,2), ..., A(M,N) (the Mth and last row). This input is achieved by a double nested loop as shown at the top of the flow chart of figure 7.2. The corresponding BASIC segment is

```
200 FOR I=1 TO M
210 FOR J=1 TO N
220 READ A(I,J)
230 NEXT J
240 NEXT I
```

It is important to have a clear mental picture of how this works. When line 200 is reached I is set to 1. At 210 J is set to 1. So at 220 the value of A(1,1) is read. When 230 is reached J is increased to 2 and the inside of the J loop is repeated, that is, the value of A(1,2) is read. This continues until the value of A(1,N) is read. Then line 230 allows control to pass through to 240. Here I is increased to 2 and the inside of the I loop is repeated, that is, the values of A(2,1), A(2,2), ..., A(2,N) are read. This continues until the values of A(M,1), A(M,2), ..., A(M,N) have been read, when 240 allows control to pass through to the next statement. It may help to visualise this process by thinking of the outer controlling variable (I) changing slowly, while the inner one (J) changes quickly; in fact J takes all its values for every value of I.

(3) Describing an algorithm for finding the largest element of a list was set as exercise 3.4. The technique is to initialise a variable B, say, to zero, then compare its value with each of the elements of the list or table; whenever a larger element is found its magnitude becomes the new value of B. In this problem we also need to store the position of the element in the table. These operations are shown in the second part of the flow chart of figure 7.2 and, as one would expect, also require a double loop. (In fact this double loop can be combined with the one used to input the matrix, thus making the algorithm more efficient. We decided to opt for simplicity - but you might like to try to redraw the flow chart to achieve the improvement.)

(4) and (5) In any exchange process in a computer program an extra storage space is needed. For example, if we need to exchange the values of P and Q then we cannot simply write

```
300 LET P=Q
310 LET Q=P
```

because at line 310 P will have its new value obtained at line 300. In fact these two statements would leave the old value of Q in both P and Q. The exchange can be made with an extra statement

```
290 LET R=P
300 LET P=Q
310 LET Q=R
```

To be convinced that this works try some values for P and Q. In our problem we have to exchange whole rows, but that is simply a matter of setting up a loop (see figure 7.2). Note that we only need a single extra variable for the exchange, because it acts only as a temporary store.

(6) Printing out a matrix is obviously similar to reading one in. The difference is the physical limitation of the paper. If the matrix has more than five columns then it is quite difficult to achieve a clear output in BASIC. To avoid further complication in this section we shall assume a maximum of five columns for the moment, and return to the problem in chapter 10.

This completes our discussion on the flow chart of figure 7.2. The corresponding BASIC program is given in figure 7.3, together with the results for the 3 by 4 matrix

$$\begin{pmatrix} 1 & 0 & 2 & -1 \\ 2 & -2 & 0 & 0 \\ -3 & 0 & -6 & 1 \end{pmatrix}$$

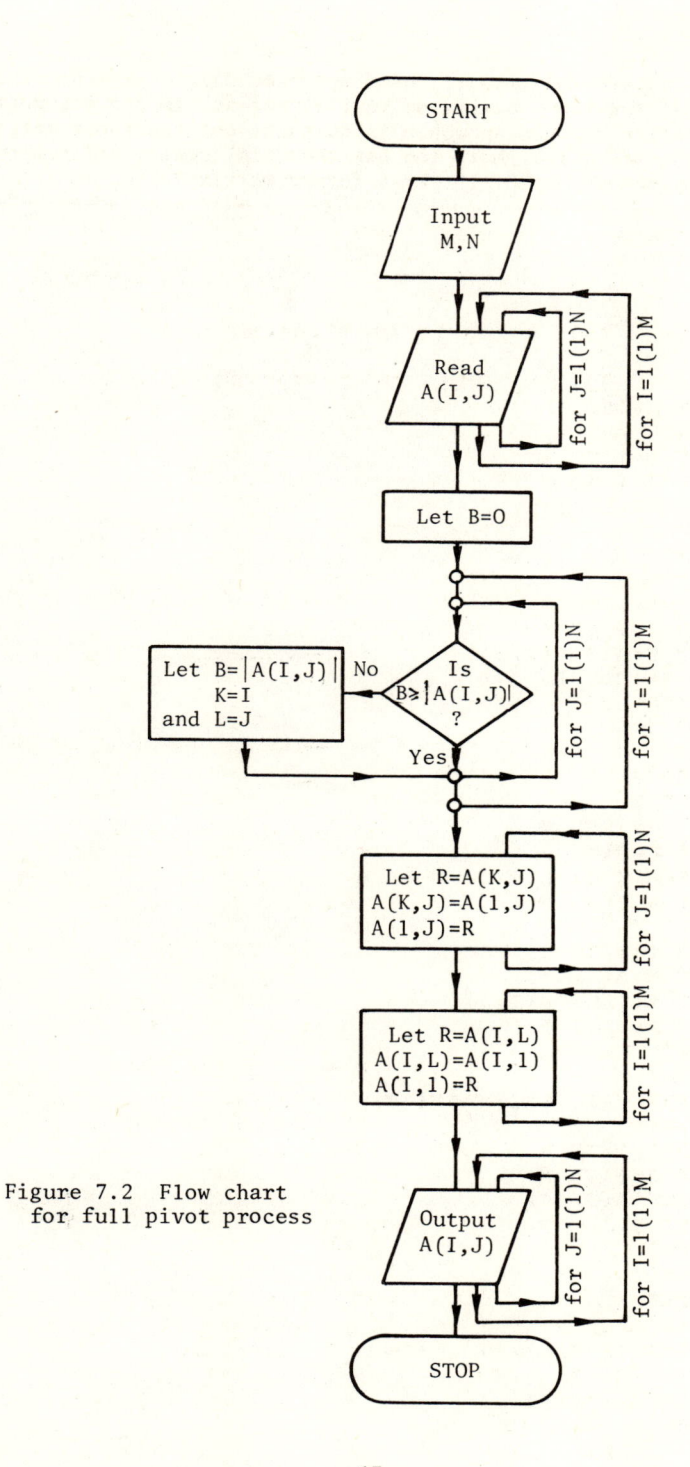

```
                    START
                      │
                      ▼
                  Input
                   M,N
                      │
                      ▼
                   Read          for J=1(1)N
                  A(I,J)         for I=1(1)M
                      │
                      ▼
                 Let B=0
                      │
                      ▼
   ┌─────────────┐ No    Is
   │Let B=|A(I,J)|├─── B≥|A(I,J)|       for J=1(1)N
   │  K=I         │       ?              for I=1(1)M
   │ and L=J      │   Yes
   └─────────────┘    │
                      ▼
               Let R=A(K,J)
               A(K,J)=A(1,J)    for J=1(1)N
               A(1,J)=R
                      │
                      ▼
               Let R=A(I,L)
               A(I,L)=A(I,1)    for I=1(1)M
               A(I,1)=R
                      │
                      ▼
                  Output         for J=1(1)N
                  A(I,J)         for I=1(1)M
                      │
                      ▼
                    STOP
```

Figure 7.2 Flow chart for full pivot process

Note how we have deliberately used separate DATA statements for each row of the input matrix so that it is easy to see its contents. An alternative to this approach is to print out the input matrix before processing it. Note too how the PRINT statements achieve the row by row output of the transformed matrix.

```
NEW OR OLD?
← OLD PIVOT
← LIST

PIVOT            ON 09/03/76 AT 18.46.03

100 REM                 FULL PIVOT PROCESS
110 DIM A(10,5)
120 READ M,N
200 FOR I=1 TO M
210 FOR J=1 TO N
220 READ A(I,J)
230 NEXT J
240 NEXT I
250 LET B=0
300 FOR I=1 TO M
310 FOR J=1 TO N
320 LET C=ABS(A(I,J))
330 IF B>=C THEN 370
340 LET B=C
350 LET K=I
360 LET L=J
370 NEXT J
380 NEXT I
400 FOR J=1 TO N
410 LET R=A(K,J)
420 LET A(K,J)=A(1,J)
430 LET A(1,J)=R
440 NEXT J
500 FOR I=1 TO M
510 LET R=A(I,L)
520 LET A(I,L)=A(I,1)
530 LET A(I,1)=R
540 NEXT I
600 PRINT
610 PRINT "PIVOTED MATRIX"
620 PRINT
630 FOR I=1 TO M
640 FOR J=1 TO N
650 PRINT A(I,J),
660 NEXT J
670 PRINT
680 NEXT I
690 PRINT
700 DATA 3,4
701 DATA  1, 0, 2,-1
702 DATA  2,-2, 0, 0
703 DATA -3, 0,-6, 1
800 END
```

← RUN

RUN PROCEEDING

PIVOTED MATRIX

-6	0	-3	1
0	-2	2	0
2	0	1	-1

FINISHED

Figure 7.3 Program for full pivot process

7.10 POSTSCRIPT

The manipulation of arrays, particularly the two-dimensional variety, is possibly the most difficult of programming skills. Like everything else in life skill comes with practice. Fortunately BASIC provides a very powerful but simple set of instructions that allow whole matrices to be manipulated (as opposed to the manipulation element by element). These matrix statements are dealt with in chapter 10, but they do not cover every possible operation that we may need - they do not include searching for largest elements or exchanging rows and columns, for example - so it is important to be able to write programs of the kind given in figure 7.3.

Lastly, we must mention that most BASIC systems allow one-dimensional *string arrays*. Such an array could, for example, store a list of names, and the list could be sorted into alphabetical order in much the same way as a list of numbers can be sorted into numerical order. This kind of application is unusual in scientific work and therefore we shall not delve into such matters. An application that might well arise is the input and subsequent output of descriptive names. Consider the analysis of pollution-measurement data for rivers. If the lead content is $A(I,J)$ for the sample taken at station I in river J, then the output of the computer analysis (whatever that might be) would be enhanced if the actual name of river J appeared, instead of just its number (J). If the string array name for the rivers is R£ we might have the following in the program

```
200 DIM A(10,10),R£(10)
210 FOR I=I TO 10
220 READ R£(I)
230 NEXT I
240 DATA "THAMES", "SEVERN","WYE",(etc.)
250 ...
```

EXERCISES

7.1 Run the program given in figure 7.1, make the alterations suggested in note (1) near the end of section 7.5, then run the program again, using any number greater than 10^6 as a terminator.

7.2 Write BASIC programs for the flow charts of exercises 3.2 and 3.5. In each case control all the loops by FOR ... NEXT statements. In the second example the list of numbers should be held in an array.

7.3 Write a BASIC program to calculate the mean $\bar{x}$ and variance s^2 of n values x_1, x_2, ..., x_n, where

$$\bar{x} = (\sum_{i=1}^{n} x_i)/n$$

and $s^2 = [(\sum_{i=1}^{n} x_i^2) - \bar{x}^2]/n$

Store the x_i values in an array; assume $n \leq 30$.

7.4 Write a BASIC program to input n and then x_1, y_1, x_2, y_2, ..., x_n, y_n, and to calculate and output the correlation coefficient

$$\rho = 1 - 6[\sum_{i=1}^{n} (x_i - y_i)^2]/n(n^2 - 1)$$

Store the x_i and y_i values in arrays; assume $n \leq 20$.

Ten variations of a chemical mixture, with steadily increasing amounts of one component, were tried out in an experiment. The required effect was measured in each case and the measurements ranked thus (treat these as the y_i values)

3, 1, 5, 4, 6, 2, 9, 10, 8, 7

Use the program to calculate the correlation coefficient expressing the correlation between the amount of the component (given by the x_i values: let them be 1, 2, ..., 10) and its effect.

7.5 Write a BASIC program to set up and print out the 4 by 4 identity matrix I, where

$$I(J, K) = \begin{cases} 1 \text{ if } J = K \\ 0 \text{ if } J \neq K \end{cases}$$

7.6 Write a BASIC program to input a square matrix of size at most 15 by 15, to divide each row of the matrix by the diagonal element in that row, and then to output the resulting matrix.

7.7 (Rather harder) Let $T(0,J)$, $J = 1(1)N$, be the trapezium rule estimate of an integral using 2^J subintervals (see section 8.1). These estimates can usually be improved by 'extrapolation to the limit' (also called Romberg integration - see Stark, chapter 6 [2]). The first extrapolates are given by

$$T(I,J) = [4T(0,J) - T(0,J-1)]/3, \quad J = 2(1)N$$

the second by

$$T(2,J) = [16T(1,J) - T(1,J-1)]/15, \quad J = 3(1)N$$

and so on, the last possible being

$$T(N-1,N) = [4^{N-1}T(N-2,N) - T(N-2,N-1)]/(4^{N-1}-1)$$

The general form is

$$T(I,J) = [4^I T(I-1,J) - T(I-1,J-1)]/(4^I-1)$$
$$J = I+1(1)N, \quad I = 1(1)N$$

Write a BASIC program to input N and $T(0,1)$, $T(0,2)$, ..., $T(0,N)$, and to calculate and output the triangular array T (shown below for N = 4).

```
T(0,1)
T(0,2)    T(1,2)
T(0,3)    T(1,3)    T(2,3)
T(0,4)    T(1,4)    T(2,4)    T(3,4)
```

Typical values of $T(0,1)$, $T(0,2)$, $T(0,3)$, ... can be seen in the right-hand column of the output from the program in figure 8.3.

8 BASIC - FUNCTIONS

8.1 CASE STUDY - NUMERICAL INTEGRATION

In chapter 4 we gave a list of standard functions available in BASIC: COS, SIN, EXP, etc. In this chapter we shall describe how to define other functions. The reason for wishing to be able to do so will become clear as the chapter progresses. To introduce the idea we shall solve a civil engineering problem.

Imagine a reservoir with a rectangular plan area A m^2, and with a weir at one end capable of discharging water at a rate of $kx^{1.5}$ m^3/s, where x m is the level of water above the weir and k is a constant. If rainwater falls on to the reservoir at a rate of q m^3/s how long will it take for the water to rise from the level of the weir to ℓ m above the weir?

The rate of increase in the volume of water in the reservoir is A dx/dt, so

$$A \frac{dx}{dt} = q - kx^{1.5}$$

therefore

$$\frac{dt}{dx} = \frac{A}{q - kx^{1.5}}$$

therefore

$$\text{rise time} = \int_0^\ell \frac{A}{q - kx^{1.5}} \, dx \qquad (8.1)$$

Now the evaluation of this integral, for given A, q, k and ℓ, is not possible by standard analytical techniques - at least, not obviously, and that is what matters - so we resort to a numerical method. Such methods are based on approximating the integrand by a simpler function, and integrating the approximation in lieu of the original. We shall use the trapezium rule, which approximates the integrand by straight-line segments - a polygonal or piecewise linear approximation (linear interpolation again!).

For example, figure 3.5 shows a polygonal approximation to a specific heat capacity as a function of temperature. Now if we wished to integrate the original function then clearly the area under the polygon gives us some kind of approximation to the true value, and the area under the polygon is made up of the areas of a set of trapezia.

Going back to our integral 8.1, suppose the polygonal approximation has n sections, with the ends of the sections being at $x = 0$, h, $2h$, ..., nh where $nh = \ell$, and, for the sake of convenience, let

$$f(x) = \frac{A}{q - kx^{1.5}}$$

Then the area of the first trapezium is

$$\tfrac{1}{2}h[f(0) + f(h)]$$

and of the second trapezium is

$$\tfrac{1}{2}h[f(h) + f(2h)]$$

and so on (see figure 8.1). Adding all such trapezoidal areas we have the approximation

$$T_n = h\,[\tfrac{1}{2}f(0) + f(h) + f(2h) + f(3h) + \ldots + f((n-1)h) + \tfrac{1}{2}f(nh)] \tag{8.2}$$

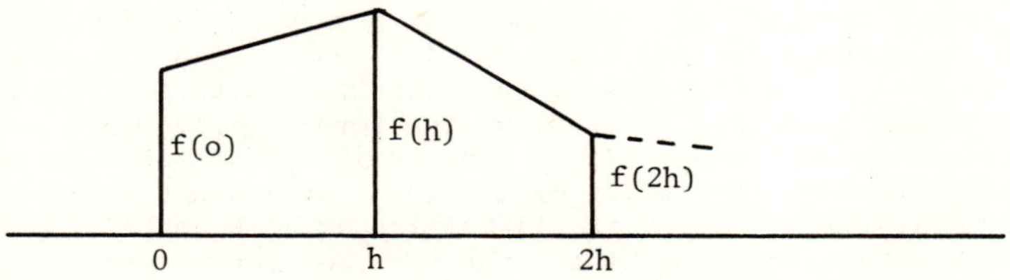

Figure 8.1 First two trapezia in compound trapezium rule

So far we have no way of assessing the error - the difference between T_n and the true value of the integral. One simple practical way of dealing with this is to halve h (that is, double the number of polygonal sections) and compare the two results T_n and T_{2n}. Better still, we can continue to halve h, calculating T_n, T_{2n}, T_{4n}, ...; this sequence will, in theory, converge to the true value of the integral, and all we need do, apparently, is stop when two successive estimates agree closely enough for our needs. In fact we shall start with T_1, which is simple $\tfrac{1}{2}\ell[f(0) + f(\ell)]$.

As a final detail we note that

$$T_{2n} = \tfrac{1}{2}h[\tfrac{1}{2}f(0) + f(\tfrac{1}{2}h) + f(h) + f(\tfrac{3}{2}h) + \ldots + f((n-\tfrac{1}{2})h) + \tfrac{1}{2}f(nh)] \tag{8.3}$$

where h is the same as in equation 8.2, that is $nh = \ell$.

Comparing equations 8.2 and 8.3 we see that

$$T_{2n} = \tfrac{1}{2}T_n + \tfrac{1}{2}h\,[f(\tfrac{1}{2}h) + f(\tfrac{3}{2}h) + f(\tfrac{5}{2}h) + \ldots + f((n-\tfrac{1}{2})h)] \tag{8.4}$$

so we can save quite a lot of time by computing T_{2n} from T_n, rather than from first principles.

The above few paragraphs are a very brief summary of the development of the trapezium rule with interval halving. For more details, and descriptions of other methods, see Stark, chapter 6 [2], although the computer programs given there are deliberately simple and therefore not very efficient.

To complete our analysis we must construct a flow chart for the method (figure 8.2). The first point to note is that we do not wish to store all the estimates T_1, T_2, T_4, ... but only need to keep the previous estimate at any time. Call the 'old' estimate T1 and the 'new' estimate T2; if H is the spacing of the N segments of the x-axis associated with the *new* estimate, then equation 8.4 becomes

$$T2 = \tfrac{1}{2}T1 + H[f(H) + f(3H) + f(5H) + \ldots + f((N-1)H)] \qquad (8.5)$$

because the h and n in equation 8.4 are associated with the *old* estimate, T_n.

The sum in equation 8.5 is constructed with a loop, f(A+IH) being added to an accumulating sum S for I = 1, 3, 5, ..., N - 1, that is, I = 1(2)N - 1. (Note that we have constructed an algorithm for the evaluation of any integral of the form $\int_A^B F(X) \, dX$, not one specifically for our problem.) The remainder of the flow chart is self-explanatory, consisting of the input of A and B and the convergence tolerance E, the initialisation of H, N and T1, the output of successive estimates and the test for convergence.

All this is supposed to be introducing functions in BASIC. Note that in the flow chart the function F appears three times, so we would normally have to write out the expression for F those three times. But if we can define F separately and refer to the definition at the three places where it is needed, then we might well save some work - particularly if F were a complicated function. Furthermore to run the program for different functions we would then have to change just the definition, and not all three occurrences in the program.

8.2 USER-DEFINED FUNCTIONS IN *BASIC*

To define our own functions within a BASIC program we use the DEF FN statement. It has the format

    DEF FNℓ(var)=function of var

where ℓ is a letter, that is, A, B, ..., Z and var is a single numeric variable. So for our case study we could write

    DEF FNI(X)=A/(Q-K*X**1.5)

Then, in the program, we can refer to the function FNI whenever needed. Specifically

```
        LET T1=0.5*H*(FNI(A)+FNI(B))
and     LET S=S+FNI(A+I*H)
```

We have chosen I in FNI to stand for integrand, but any other choice is possible. Also, the X in the DEF FN statement is a dummy variable so

```
        DEF FNV(W)=A/(Q-K*W**1.5)
        LET T1=0.5*H*(FNV(A)+FNV(B))
and     LET S=S+FNV(A+I*H)
```

say, would have exactly the same effect. Note that the function on the right of the equals sign in the DEF FN statement can include variables other than the dummy variable. These variables take the value they have at the time that the function is referenced.

8.3 CHECK YOUR PROGRESS

This question will test the understanding of the DEF FN statement. What would be the value printed at line 150 in the following program?

```
        100 DEF FNP(A)=X/(X*X+A*A)
        110 DEF FNQ(A)=A/(X*X+A*A)
        120 LET X=-1
        130 LET Y=FNP(X)
        140 LET X=FNQ(Y)
        150 PRINT X
        160 END
```

Answer

-0.4 (Hint: FNP(X)=X/(X*X+X*X))

8.4 A PROGRAM FOR THE CASE STUDY

Having introduced the DEF FN statement we can program the flow chart of figure 8.2 immediately. Our version is shown in figure 8.3. Note again the detailed output, which makes it so much easier to use the program.

This is a good example for which to design test problems. How can we be sure that the program is correct? The obvious answer is to use it to evaluate some integrals whose values are already known to us, ones for which the successive estimates by the trapezium rule can easily be calculated by hand. For example

$$\int_0^1 x^2 \, dx = \frac{1}{3}$$

and $T_1 = 1[\frac{1}{2}(0)^2 + \frac{1}{2}(1)^2] = 0.5$

$T_2 = \frac{1}{2}T_1 + \frac{1}{2}[(\frac{1}{2})^2] = 0.375$

$T_4 = \frac{1}{2}T_2 + \frac{1}{4}[(\frac{1}{4})^2 + (\frac{3}{4})^2] = 0.34375$

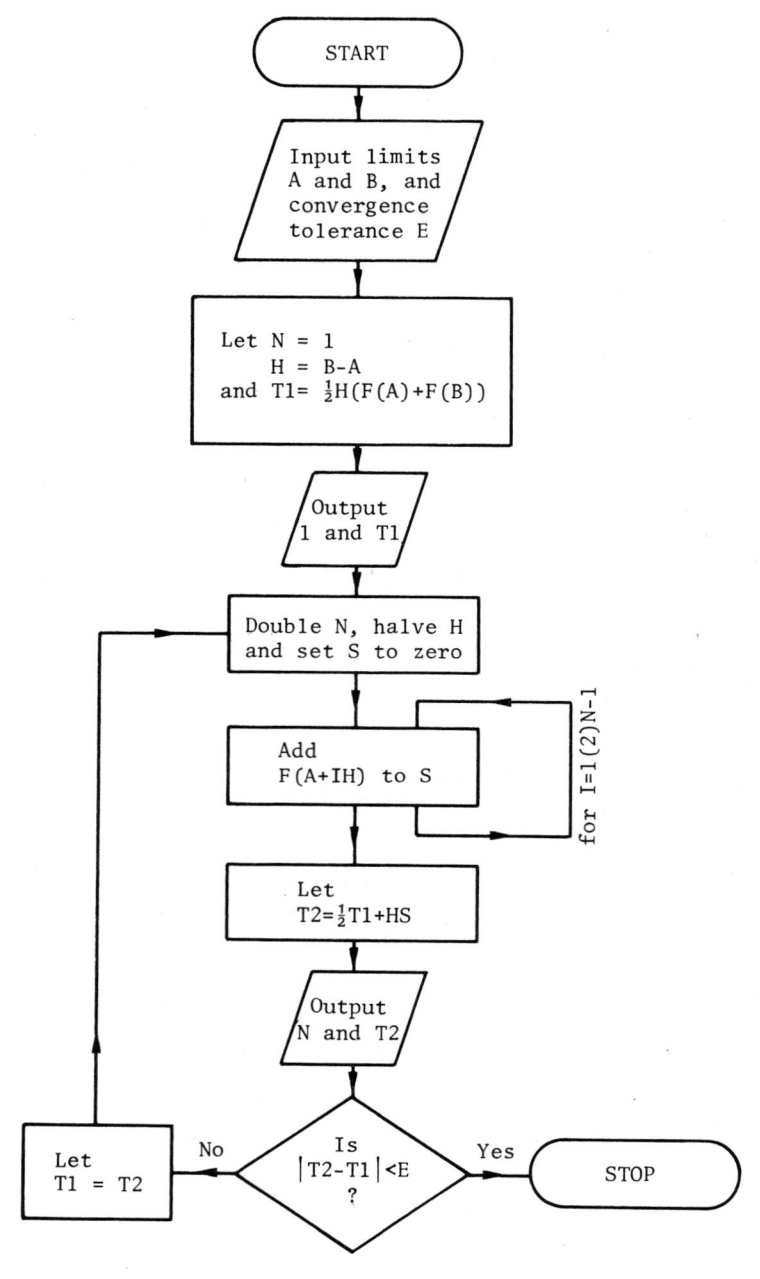

```
                    ┌─────────┐
                    │  START  │
                    └────┬────┘
                         ↓
                ╱────────────────╱
               ╱ Input limits   ╱
              ╱  A and B, and  ╱
             ╱  convergence   ╱
            ╱   tolerance E  ╱
            ────────────────
                         ↓
              ┌──────────────────────┐
              │ Let N = 1            │
              │     H = B-A          │
              │ and T1= ½H(F(A)+F(B))│
              └──────────┬───────────┘
                         ↓
                   ╱──────────╱
                  ╱ Output   ╱
                 ╱ 1 and T1 ╱
                 ──────────
                         ↓
              ┌──────────────────────┐
         →    │ Double N, halve H    │
         │    │ and set S to zero    │
         │    └──────────┬───────────┘
         │               ↓
         │    ┌──────────────────┐
         │    │      Add         │  ⟲ for I=1(2)N-1
         │    │  F(A+IH) to S    │
         │    └──────────┬───────┘
         │               ↓
         │    ┌──────────────────┐
         │    │     Let          │
         │    │  T2=½T1+HS       │
         │    └──────────┬───────┘
         │               ↓
         │         ╱──────────╱
         │        ╱ Output   ╱
         │       ╱ N and T2 ╱
         │       ──────────
         │               ↓
         │          ╱─────────╲
    ┌────────┐ No  ╱   Is      ╲ Yes   ┌────────┐
    │  Let   │←───⟨  |T2-T1|<E  ⟩─────→│  STOP  │
    │ T1 = T2│     ╲      ?    ╱       └────────┘
    └────────┘      ╲─────────╱
```

Figure 8.2   Flow chart for trapezium rule

By specifying a convergence tolerance of about 0.005 we should get the above three estimates, and a few more, the last two differing by less than 0.005.

In figure 8.3 the results are, of course, for our case study. The data used are as follows: $A = 4000$ m^2, $q = 10$ m^3/s, $k = 20$, $\ell = 0.4$ m, and the convergence tolerance = 0.1 (pretty well guaranteeing accuracy to the nearest second).

```
NEW OR OLD?
← OLD TRAPINT
← LIST

TRAPINT        ON 09/03/76 AT 18.53.02

101 REM              TRAPEZIUM RULE INTEGRATION
102 REM               WITH INTERVAL HALVING
110 DEF FNI(X)=400/(1-2*X**1.5)
120 PRINT "TYPE LOWER AND UPPER LIMITS OF INTEGRATION"
121 PRINT "IN THE FORM A,B";
130 INPUT A,B
140 PRINT
150 PRINT "TYPE MAXIMUM ACCEPTABLE DIFFERENCE BETWEEN"
151 PRINT "SUCCESSIVE ESTIMATES";
160 INPUT E
170 PRINT
180 PRINT "NO. OF","ESTIMATE OF"
181 PRINT "SUBINTERVALS","INTEGRAL"
190 PRINT
200 LET N=1
210 LET H=B-A
220 LET T1=0.5*H*(FNI(A)+FNI(B))
230 PRINT 1,T1
300 LET N=2*N
310 LET H=0.5*H
320 LET S=0
330 FOR I=1 TO N-1 STEP 2
340 LET S=S+FNI(A+I*H)
350 NEXT I
360 LET T2=0.5*T1+H*S
370 PRINT N,T2
380 IF ABS(T2-T1)<E THEN 500
390 LET T1=T2
400 GO TO 300
500 END
```

```
← RUN
              RUN PROCEEDING
TYPE LOWER AND UPPER LIMITS OF INTEGRATION
IN THE FORM A,B← 0,0.4

TYPE MAXIMUM ACCEPTABLE DIFFERENCE BETWEEN
SUCCESSIVE ESTIMATES← 0.1

NO. OF              ESTIMATE OF
SUBINTERVALS        INTEGRAL

    1               160
    2               177.429
    4               190.995
    8               199.388
   16               204.035
   32               206.476
   64               207.726
  128               208.358
  256               208.676
  512               208.836
 1024               208.916

             ·FINISHED
```

Figure 8.3 Program for trapezium rule

8.5 A SECOND CASE STUDY - SOLVING AN EQUATION

A control system - the classic mechanical example is a steam engine controlled by a governor - is characterised by the response of the system to various inputs or perturbations. These reponses can be predicted by solving the differential equation(s) describing the behaviour of the system, and the critical part of the solution is the so-called complementary function. When the differential equation is linear, with constant coefficients, this complementary function depends in a simple way on the solutions of the related algebraic auxiliary equation.

If the solution of differential equations is not familiar it will not really spoil our example, just keep on reading. The particular differential equation we shall consider is

$$\frac{d^3x}{dt^3} + \frac{d^2x}{dt^2} + 0.01 \frac{dx}{dt} + x = 0$$

and the corresponding auxiliary equation is

$$m^3 + m^2 + 0.01m + 1 = 0 \tag{8.6}$$

If this equation has any positive solutions, or complex solutions with positive real parts, then the control system will have a response including an increasing exponential factor, that is, it will be unstable. So our problem reduces to finding all three solutions of the cubic equation 8.6.

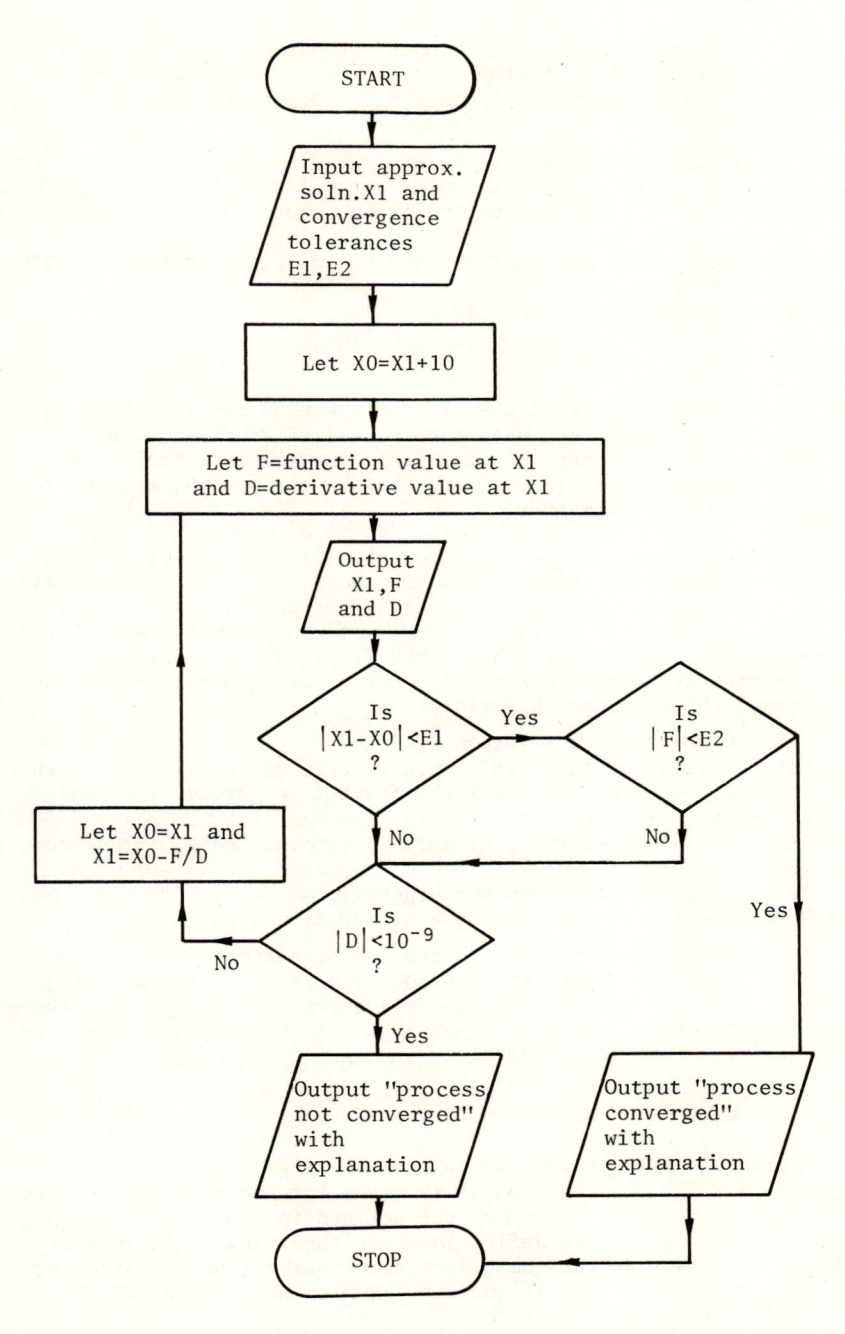

```
                    ┌─────────┐
                    │  START  │
                    └────┬────┘
                         ↓
                  ╱──────────────╲
                 ╱ Input approx.  ╲
                ╱  soln. X1 and    ╲
                ╲  convergence     ╱
                 ╲ tolerances     ╱
                  ╲ E1,E2        ╱
                   ╲────┬───────╱
                        ↓
                ┌───────────────┐
                │ Let X0=X1+10  │
                └───────┬───────┘
                        ↓
        ┌──────────────────────────────────┐
        │ Let F=function value at X1       │
        │ and D=derivative value at X1     │
        └────────────────┬─────────────────┘
                         ↓
                   ╱──────────╲
                  ╱  Output    ╲
                  ╲  X1,F      ╱
                   ╲  and D   ╱
                    ╲────┬───╱
                         ↓
                      ╱─────╲         ╱─────╲
                     ╱  Is   ╲  Yes  ╱  Is   ╲
                    ╱ |X1-X0|╲──────╱  |F|<E2 ╲
                    ╲  <E1   ╱      ╲    ?    ╱
                     ╲  ?   ╱        ╲───┬───╱
                      ╲─┬──╱             │ No
                        │ No             │
    ┌─────────────┐     ↓                ↓
    │Let X0=X1 and│  ╱─────╲
    │X1=X0-F/D    │ ╱  Is   ╲                          Yes
    └──────▲──────┘╱  |D|   ╲
           │      ╲ <10⁻⁹  ╱
       No  │       ╲  ?   ╱
           └────────╲─┬──╱
                     ↓ Yes
    ╱──────────────╲        ╱──────────────╲
   ╱Output "process ╲      ╱Output "process ╲
  ╱ not converged"  ╲     ╱  converged"     ╲
  ╲    with         ╱     ╲    with         ╱
   ╲ explanation   ╱       ╲ explanation   ╱
    ╲──────┬──────╱         ╲──────┬──────╱
           ↓                       ↓
        ┌──────┐
        │ STOP │←──────────────────┘
        └──────┘
```

Figure 8.4 Flow chart for Newton's method

Now the most popular of the simple methods for solving equations such as equation 8.6 is Newton's method; again refer to Stark [2] for the details, this time in chapter 3. Briefly, one version is as follows.

(1) Find an approximate solution x_0.
(2) Calculate a new approximation x_1 by $x_1 = x_0 - f(x_0)/f'(x_0)$, where $f(x) = 0$ is the equation being solved and f' is the derivative of f.
(3) If x_0 and x_1 are sufficiently close, *and* $f(x_1)$ is sufficiently small, stop.
(4) Otherwise let $x_0 = x_1$ and go to (2).

Notes

(a) If $f'(x_0)$ is too small then Newton's method can fail. In our version we shall terminate the process if $|f'(x_0)| < 10^{-9}$.
(b) The convergence test, (3) above, is our personal choice, and not the only possible one. We shall return to the reasons for it later in the chapter.

Figure 8.4 shows a flow chart for this algorithm. It appears to differ quite considerably from the above but is really very close to it. The problem to solve in setting out the algorithm in detail is where to start the iteration loop. If we follow the above steps closely, then, in order to check that $f(x_1)$ is small enough at step (3), we find that the algorithm becomes rather clumsy. So we have rearranged the sequence as follows.

(1) Find an approximate solution x_1.
(2) Let the value of the 'old' approximation x_0 be $x_1 + 10$, so that $|x_1 - x_0|$ will not be small the first time through the loop.
(3) Calculate $F = f(x_1)$ and $D = f'(x_1)$.
(4) If $|x_1 - x_0| <$ tolerance E1 *and* $|F| <$ tolerance E2, stop (convergence).
(5) If $|D| < 10^{-9}$, stop (non-convergence).
(6) Otherwise let $x_0 = x_1$ and $x_1 = x_0 - F/D$, and go to (3).

Considerable insight into the process of setting up algorithms would be gained by trying to construct a version of the algorithm, starting from the four basic steps given previously (that is, those just before notes (a) and (b) above). Then it will be seen why we have preferred the second version.

8.6 A PROGRAM FOR NEWTON'S METHOD

The coding in BASIC of the flow chart of figure 8.4 is shown in figure 8.5. The important point to note, for the purposes of this chapter, is that $f(x)$ and $f'(x)$ are defined in the DEF FN statements 110 and 120; these definitions are then used in statements 310 and 320. So, in this case, the functions are used just once, and one could argue that it would be simpler not to use DEF FN statements at all but to write

```
310 LET F=X1**3+X1*X1+0.01*X1+1
320 LET D=3*X1*X1+2*X1+0.01
```

However, we believe that it is more elegant to define the functions as we have and that it is easier to modify the program to solve a different equation if the function and its derivative are so defined.

Figure 8.5 also shows the results for the case study. (The initial approximation x = -1.5 was found by a little trial and error.) Since m = -1.4614 is a solution we can factorise the left-hand side of equation 8.6, obtaining

$$(m + 1.4614)(m^2 - 0.4614m + 0.68428) = 0$$

```
NEW OR OLD?
← OLD NEWTSOL
← LIST

NEWTSOL          ON 09/03/76 AT 19.04.10

100 REM             SOLN. OF AN EQN. BY NEWTON'S METHOD
110 DEF FNF(X)=X**3+X*X+0.01*X+1
120 DEF FND(X)=3*X*X+2*X+0.01
130 PRINT
140 PRINT "TYPE INITIAL APPROX. TO SOLN.";
150 INPUT X1
160 PRINT
170 PRINT "TYPE MAX. ACCEPTABLE DIFF. BETWEEN"
171 PRINT "SUCCESSIVE ESTIMATES";
180 INPUT E1
190 PRINT
200 PRINT "TYPE MAX. ACCEPTABLE VALUE OF FUNCTION";
210 INPUT E2
220 PRINT
230 PRINT "     X","    F(X)","   DF(X)"
240 PRINT
250 LET X0=X1+10
300 REM           START ITERATION LOOP
310 LET F=FNF(X1)
320 LET D=FND(X1)
330 PRINT X1,F,D
340 IF ABS(X1-X0)>=E1 THEN 360
350 IF ABS(F)<E2 THEN 400
360 IF ABS(D)<1E-9 THEN 500
370 LET X0=X1
380 LET X1=X0-F/D
390 GO TO 310
400 PRINT
401 PRINT "PROCESS CONVERGED: DIFF. BETWEEN"
402 PRINT "SUCCESSIVE ESTIMATES, AND FUNCTION"
403 PRINT "VALUE, BOTH LESS THAN ACCEPTABLE MAX."
404 PRINT
410 GO TO 600
500 PRINT
501 PRINT "PROCESS NOT CONVERGED: DERIVATIVE"
502 PRINT "VALUE TOO SMALL"
503 PRINT
600 END
```

```
← RUN
              RUN PROCEEDING

TYPE INITIAL APPROX. TO SOLN.← -1.5

TYPE MAX. ACCEPTABLE DIFF. BETWEEN
SUCCESSIVE ESTIMATES← 5E-7

TYPE MAX. ACCEPTABLE VALUE OF FUNCTION← 5E-7

        X              F(X)            DF(X)

   -1.5            -.14              3.76
   -1.46277        -.004801          3.50352
   -1.4614         -.000006          3.49424
   -1.46139        -.145519E-10      3.49423
   -1.46139        -.145519E-10      3.49423

PROCESS CONVERGED: DIFF. BETWEEN
SUCCESSIVE ESTIMATES, AND FUNCTION
VALUE, BOTH LESS THAN ACCEPTABLE MAX.


              FINISHED
```

Figure 8.5 Program for Newton's method

So the other two solutions can be found from $m^2 - 0.4614m + 0.68428 = 0$, and are $m = \frac{1}{2}(0.4614 \pm 1.5888j)$, where $j^2 = -1$. The positive real part of these two solutions implies that the control system would be unstable.

The program for Newton's method is also one for which it is interesting to design test problems. It is easy to design a straightforward example, such as

$$(x - 1)(x^2 + 1) = 0$$

which has one real solution at $x = 1$. Using an initial approximation of, say, $x = 0.5$ will quickly show whether the essence of the program is correct. To check that the convergence and non-convergence tests are working properly is a little harder. Here are some possible test cases.

(a) $(x - 1)^{20} = 0$ with initial approximation $x = 1.1$ and both convergence tolerances set to 10^{-30}. This tests the check on the derivative because $|20(x - 1)^{19}| = 2 \times 10^{-19} < 10^{-9}$ when $x = 1.1$.
(b) $10^6 x^2 - 1 = 0$ with initial approximation $x = 0.1$ and both convergence tolerances set to 0.05. This tests that, even though $|X1 - X0| < E1$ after a few iterations (because the successive estimates quickly converge towards the solution 0.001), the program waits until $|F| < E2$, $|F|$ being large initially.
(c) $10^{-6} x^2 - 1 = 0$ with initial approximation $x = 2000$ and both convergence tolerances set to 0.05. This produces the reverse

condition to that in (b). $|F|$ becomes small quickly but $|X1 - X0|$ decreases slowly.

Running the Newton's method program with these examples will give good practice at changing the DEF FN statements. As an example of how Newton's method can behave quite peculiarly, for the first few iterations at least, try the case study example with an initial approximation of x = -0.5.

EXERCISES

8.1 Write a BASIC program to tabulate a function f(x) for x = a(h)b (that is, x = a, a + h, a + 2h, ..., b). Define f in a DEF FN statement, and treat a, h and b as input data.

8.2 A function of two variables can be defined thus

    DEF FNA(X)=1+X+Y+X*Y

To evaluate the function the required value of X appears as usual but the required value of Y has to be assigned separately before the function is used; for example

    300 LET Y=3
    310 PRINT FNA(2)

outputs the value 12 (that is, 1 + 2 + 3 + 2 * 3). Use this device to write a program to tabulate a function of two variables.

8.3 Draw a flow chart and write a BASIC program for the bisection method for solving equations. If the equation is f(x) = 0 and a solution is known to exist in the interval a < x < b then this method slowly but surely approaches the solution by continuously bisecting the interval, as follows.

(i) Let c = $\frac{1}{2}$(a + b);
(ii) If f(a)f(c) < 0 let b = c, otherwise let a = c;
(iii) Go to (i)

(It is a good idea to print out a, b and c after step (i), each time through the loop.) The loop should be executed n times, where n is the smallest integer such that $(b - a)/2^n$ is less than the accuracy required in the solution. Use a DEF FN statement to define f and treat a, b and n as input data.

8.4 Differential equations of the form dy/dx = f(x, y), with y = y_0 when x = x_0, are usually solved numerically by a step-by-step method that finds approximate values y_1, y_2, y_3, ... for y at values $x_0 + h$, $x_0 + 2h$, $x_0 + 3h$, ... for x, where h is some predetermined step-length. One such method is the Runge-Kutta method of order 2, in which the recurrence relation is

$$y_{i+1} = y_i + \tfrac{1}{2}h(k_1 + k_2)$$

where $k_1 = f(x_i, y_i)$ and $k_2 = f(x_i + h, y_i + hk_1)$.

Draw a flow chart and write a BASIC program to do N steps of this method, given N, h, x_0 and y_0 as input data and defining f in a DEF FN statement. (See exercise 8.2 for how to deal with functions of two variables.)

Apply the program to the equation $dy/dx = x + y$, with $y = 0$ when $x = 0$, doing N = 10 steps of length h = 0.1. (The true solution is $y = e^x - 1 - x$.) Note that it is not necessary to store the x and y values in arrays since the recurrence relations can be thought of as

$$y_{new} = y_{old} + \tfrac{1}{2}h(k_1 + k_2)$$
$$x_{new} = x_{old} + h$$
$$k_1 = f(x_{old}, y_{old})$$
$$k_2 = f(x_{new}, y_{old} + hk_1)$$

so that only two x and two y values need be stored at any one time.

9 BASIC - SUBROUTINES

9.1 CASE STUDY - MORE NUMERICAL INTEGRATION

In the previous chapter we constructed a program for the trapezium rule in which the function to be integrated appeared three times. To avoid writing out the function those three times we used the DEF FN statement to define the function, and referred to that definition at the three places in the program where it was needed.

This was a simple example of the more general concept of a subroutine - that is, a segment of program that is separate from but used by the main part of the program. Normally the subroutine is referred to more than once by the main part of the program, otherwise it is rarely worth writing the subroutine separately.

As our first example of this idea we shall construct a generalisation of the trapezium rule program. So far we have assumed that the integrand is given by a single formula, but this is not always the case. As a specific example, consider the calculation of the energy required to compress a spring system with preloading at various points. The energy is the integral of the force required, integrated over the path moved by the point of application, and the force will be given by different formulae for different parts of the displacement: one formula for the displacement from zero to the overcoming of the first preload point, another for the displacement from there to the second preload point, and so on. The integral to be evaluated in such a situation has the form

$$\int_{a_0}^{a_n} f = \int_{a_0}^{a_1} f_1 + \int_{a_1}^{a_2} f_2 + \ldots + \int_{a_{n-1}}^{a_n} f_n$$

where $a_1, a_2, \ldots, a_{n-1}$ are the points at which the integrand f changes from one form to the next, and f_i is the form of f between a_{i-1} and a_i.

To avoid the difficulty of setting up a physical example that is sufficiently complicated to need a computer program for its evaluation, we shall consider a mathematical example of the same form. Specifically we shall evaluate

$$\int_0^1 f$$

where

$$f(x) = \begin{cases} \sin(\pi x^2) & 0 \leq x \leq \tfrac{1}{2} \\ \sin(\pi/16 x^2) & \tfrac{1}{2} \leq x \leq 1 \end{cases}$$

It is clear that to evaluate f(x) we shall need an IF statement to discover whether $0 \leq x \leq \tfrac{1}{2}$ or $\tfrac{1}{2} \leq x \leq 1$. Although this situation cannot be dealt with by a single DEF FN statement it is possible to deal with it using two DEF FN statements, with the IF statement to choose between them at each of the three occurrences of the function. However, we shall prefer to use the subroutine concept. The program can then be adapted very easily to deal with any explicit form of the integrand simply by rewriting the subroutine.

Here is the subroutine for our example

```
450 IF X < 0.5 THEN 480
460 LET F=SIN(0.1963495/(X*X))
470 GO TO 490
480 LET F=SIN(3.141593*X*X)
490 .....
```

In the next section we shall describe how the main part of the program 'calls' the subroutine, and how control is returned from the subroutine to the main part.

9.2 SUBROUTINES IN *BASIC*

Referring to the trapezium rule program in figure 8.3 let us consider the calculation of the function value at line 340

```
340 LET S=S+FNI(A+I*H)
```

In the DEF FN statement 110

```
110 DEF FNI(X)=400/(1-2*X**1.5)
```

we defined the function by its effect on a dummy quantity X; the same approach has, of course, been used in our subroutine in the previous section. Although we can fix the value of X required when we refer to a defined function - for example FNI(A+I*H) in line 340 - this is not possible when we call a subroutine. In fact the call is simply

   GOSUB line no.

where line no. is the number of the first statement of the subroutine. So, in our case, we shall always have

   GOSUB 450

This means that we shall have to set the value of X in an assignment statement before calling the subroutine by the GOSUB statement.

So, in place of line 340 shown above, we shall have to substitute

```
340 LET X=A+I*H
343 GOSUB 450
346 LET S=S+F
```

F being the variable containing the function value returned by the subroutine, (see lines 460 and 480 of the subroutine). But how does the subroutine return that value? The first requirement is that the position of the end of the subroutine must be clear, and it is marked, quite naturally, by the

RETURN

statement. This would be line 490 in our example. When the RETURN statement is encountered control is transferred to the statement after the GOSUB that last called the subroutine.

The GOSUB and RETURN statements are the only new statements required for using subroutines in BASIC.

9.3 A PROGRAM FOR THE CASE STUDY

We have dealt above with the appearance of the integrand at line 340 in figure 8.3; now we must consider those in line 220

```
220 LET T1=0.5*H*(FNI(A)+FNI(B))
```

There are two function references here so two GOSUB statements are needed. We shall replace line 220 by

```
220 LET X=A
221 GOSUB 450
222 LET T1=F
223 LET X=B
224 GOSUB 450
225 LET T1=0.5*H*(T1+F)
```

Note how we have avoided using a new temporary storage variable by holding what was FNI(A) in T1 until FNI(B) has been calculated.

This completes our preparation. As an example of how programs can be modified figure 9.1 shows the alteration of our previous trapezium rule program (figure 8.3), its storage, and a run giving the value of the integral discussed in section 9.1. Note that we have used two new commands - RENAME and DELETE. The first of these gives the program a new name for storage purposes - we cannot usually SAVE the new version with the same name as the old one. The DELETE command removes the statements with the numbers given after it.

```
NEW OR OLD?
← OLD TRAPINT
← 220 LET X=A
← 221 GOSUB 450
← 222 LET T1=F
← 223 LET X=B
← 224 GOSUB 450
← 225 LET T1=0.5*H*(T1+F)
← 340 LET X=A+I*H
← 343 GOSUB 450
← 346 LET S=S+F
← 450 IF X<0.5 THEN 480
← 460 LET F=SIN(0.1963495/(X*X))
← 470 GO TO 490
← 480 LET F=SIN(3.141593*X*X)
← 490 RETURN
← DELETE 110
← RENAME TRAPSUB
← SAVE

← RUN
                RUN PROCEEDING
TYPE LOWER AND UPPER LIMITS OF INTEGRATION
IN THE FORM A,B← 0,1

TYPE MAXIMUM ACCEPTABLE DIFFERENCE BETWEEN
SUCCESSIVE ESTIMATES← 5E-5

NO. OF            ESTIMATE OF
SUBINTERVALS      INTEGRAL

   1              .097545
   2              .402326
   4              .335441
   8              .319224
  16              .315231
  32              .314238
  64              .313991
 128              .313929
 256              .313913

              FINISHED
```

Figure 9.1 Incorporation of subroutine into
         trapezium rule program

9.4 CHECK YOUR PROGRESS

Here is an example of the use of a subroutine. What would be the value of C printed at line 190?

```
100 READ N,R
110 LET I=N-R+1
120 LET J=N
130 GOSUB 500
140 LET C=Z
```

```
150 LET I=1
160 LET J=R
170 GOSUB 500
180 LET C=C/Z
190 PRINT C
200 GO TO 999
500 LET Z=1
510 FOR K=I TO J
520 LET Z=Z*K
530 NEXT K
540 RETURN
900 DATA 6,2
999 END
```

The answer is 15. (What well-known mathematical quantity is the program evaluating?) Note the need for a GO TO before the first line of the subroutine to avoid executing the latter unnecessarily.

9.5 A SECOND CASE STUDY - A QUEUEING PROBLEM

Here is another calculation containing a subcalculation that occurs more than once, and that can usefully be written as a subroutine.

Imagine a skilled machinist employed to do 'one-off' jobs. The jobs arrive at his work station in a random fashion, with the average time between arrivals calculated as one-and-a-quarter hours. The time that the machinist takes to do each job consists of quarter-hour minimum setting-up time plus a time that is assumed to be random but that averages 1 hour.

The job arrival intervals and the machining times (above the initial quarter-hour) form what statisticians call exponential distributions, that is, the probability that the interval between two arrivals will be less than or equal to t is $p = 1 - \exp(-t/\lambda)$, where λ is the average arrival interval, and the probability that a job requires a time less than or equal to t for machining is given by the same expression, except that λ is then the average machining time. We can simulate a sequence of arrival intervals and machining times from the expression $t_i = -\lambda \log_e(1 - p_i)$ (obtained by rearranging the expression above for p in terms of t), by allowing p_i to be a sequence of values obtained from a random-number generator. (More can be found about queue simulation in Hillier and Lieberman, chapter 14 [3].) In fact, if the p_i are random and $0 < p_i < 1$ then the $1 - p_i$ are also random and satisfy $0 < 1 - p_i < 1$, so we shall use the expression $t_i = -\lambda \log_e p_i$.

With this initial information we can write a computer program that simulates what might happen at the machine. We shall choose to calculate an average waiting time for the arriving jobs, but many other experiments are possible.

The program to do this is quite short. A flow chart is shown in figure 9.2 (note that the subroutine has a separate flow chart), and here are some notes of explanation.

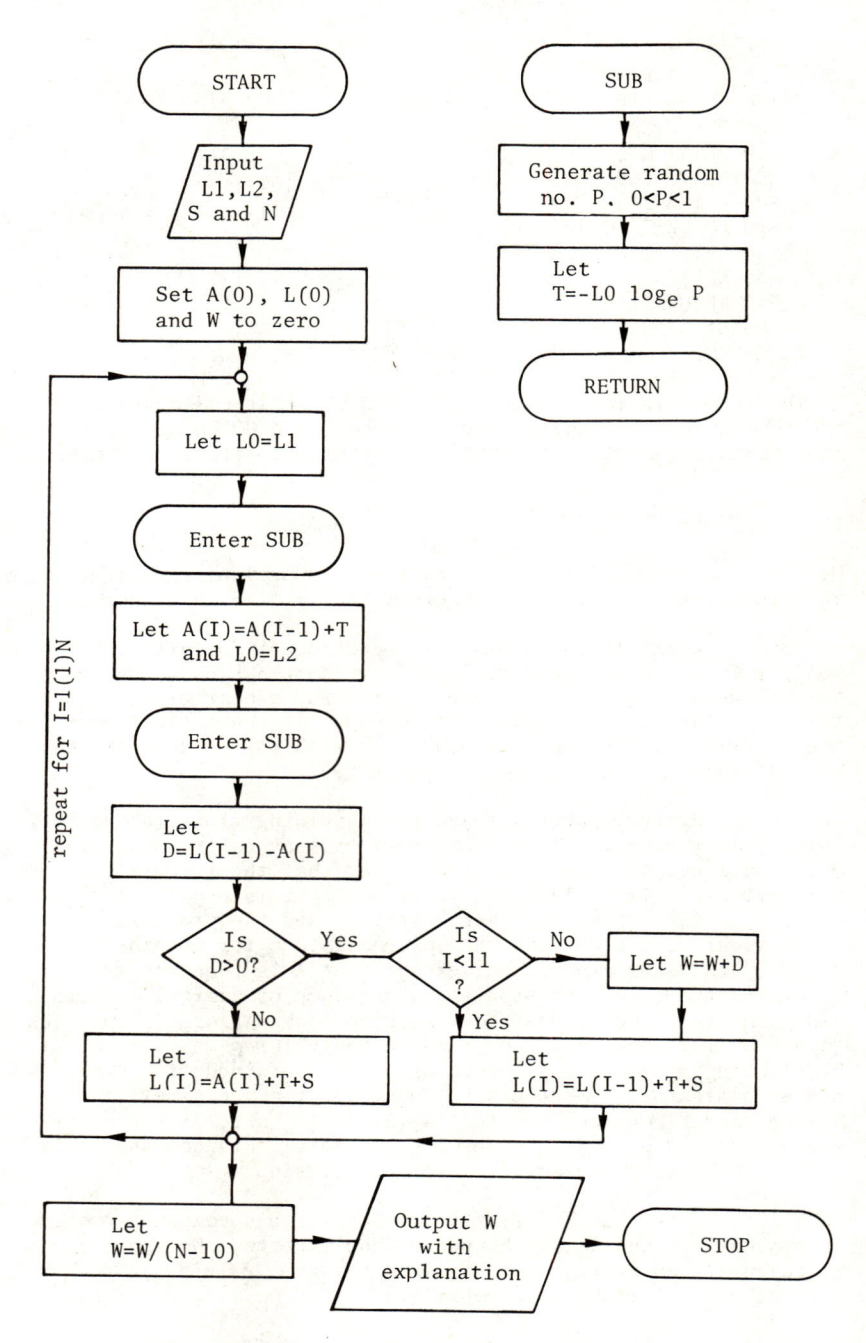

```
                START                          SUB
                  │                             │
                  ▼                             ▼
              ┌────────┐              ┌──────────────────┐
              │ Input  │              │ Generate random  │
              │ L1,L2, │              │ no. P. 0<P<1     │
              │ S and N│              └──────────────────┘
              └────────┘                       │
                  │                            ▼
                  ▼                    ┌──────────────┐
        ┌──────────────────┐           │ Let          │
        │ Set A(0), L(0)   │           │ T=-L0 log_e P│
        │ and W to zero    │           └──────────────┘
        └──────────────────┘                   │
                  │                            ▼
                  ▼                        RETURN
             ┌──────────┐
             │Let L0=L1 │
             └──────────┘
                  │
                  ▼
            ┌───────────┐
            │ Enter SUB │
            └───────────┘
                  │
                  ▼
         ┌──────────────────┐
         │Let A(I)=A(I-1)+T │
         │and L0=L2         │
         └──────────────────┘
                  │
                  ▼
            ┌───────────┐
            │ Enter SUB │
            └───────────┘
                  │
                  ▼
          ┌──────────────┐
          │ Let          │
          │ D=L(I-1)-A(I)│
          └──────────────┘
                  │
                  ▼
               Is D>0? ──Yes──► Is I<11? ──No──► Let W=W+D
                  │                │
                  │No              │Yes
                  ▼                ▼
         ┌──────────────────┐  ┌──────────────────────┐
         │ Let              │  │ Let                  │
         │ L(I)=A(I)+T+S    │  │ L(I)=L(I-1)+T+S      │
         └──────────────────┘  └──────────────────────┘

    repeat for I=1(1)N

         ┌──────────────┐    ┌──────────────┐
         │ Let          │    │ Output W     │
         │ W=W/(N-10)   │──► │ with         │──► STOP
         └──────────────┘    │ explanation  │
                             └──────────────┘
```

Fig 9.2   Flow chart for queueing problem

The main part of the flow chart starts with the input of the average time between job arrivals (L1) and the average time (above minimum setting-up time) to complete jobs (L2); also to be input are the minimum setting-up time itself (S) and the number of jobs to be considered in a particular program run (N). Next the summation accumulator W is set to zero, along with A(0) and L(0). Now A(I) and L(I) are to be the actual arrival and completion times of the Ith job, and, to avoid calculating A(1) and L(1) separately from A(2), L(2), ..., A(N), L(N), we are using the fact that A(0) and L(0) do exist in some BASIC systems. When I is greater than one A(I) is just A(I - 1) plus a random arrival interval, but A(1) is *zero* plus a random arrival interval; so if A(0) exists and is set to zero then A(1) is A(0) plus a random arrival interval and this has the same form as the calculation of A(2), ..., A(N). If A(0) does not exist in the BASIC system it will be necessary to calculate A(1) separately, thus

(1) Let L0=L1
(2) Enter SUB
(3) Let A(1)=T

similarly for L(1)

(1) Let L0=L2
(2) Enter SUB
(3) Let L(1)=A(1)+T+S

In this case the loop in the flow chart will be executed for I = 2(1)N instead of I = 1(1)N.

There is a complication to the calculation of L(I): it will be L(I - 1) + T + S if the Ith job is waiting in the queue, but A(I) + T + S if the machinist has to wait for it to arrive. To distinguish between these two cases we compute the waiting time of the Ith job: L(I - 1) - A(I). If this is negative the Ith job has not arrived yet! If it is positive we are not only able to choose the correct form for L(I) but also to add the waiting time to W preparatory to calculating the average waiting time. One last complication: until the system has been working for some time its behaviour tends to show transient effects; therefore we have (arbitrarily) chosen not to include the waiting times (if any) of the first ten jobs.

9.6 A PROGRAM FOR THE QUEUEING PROBLEM

Figure 9.2 is very close to being a BASIC program already. Figure 9.3 shows an actual program for the queueing problem, with a result based on the data described in section 9.3, namely L1 = 1.25, L2 = 1, S = 0.25. We have chosen N = 50 to complete the input of data; that is, to simulate the passage of fifty jobs through the system. It is important to state here that we are *not* suggesting that the average waiting time obtained by this one run of the program has any significance by itself. More information on queueing theory and the simulation of queues will be found in Hillier and Lieberman [3].

The only aspect of the program worth expanding on is the use of the function RND to generate the random numbers. In the current ICL version of this function RND(X) is based on the time of day if X < 0, on the number previously generated if X = 0 (on a fixed number if RND has not been used previously), and on X itself if X > 0. To obtain a different sequence of random numbers on each run of the program it is therefore necessary to 'seed' the function initially by calculating RND(-1), say, (see line 200 of figure 9.3) and to use RND(0) thereafter (line 900). Before applying it, establish how RND is used in your own BASIC system.

```
NEW OR OLD?
← OLD QUEUE
← LIST

QUEUE           ON 16/03/76 AT 19.10.03

100 REM QUEUEING PROBLEM
110 DIM A(50),L(50)
120 PRINT "INPUT MEAN ARRIVAL INTERVAL (HRS)";
130 INPUT L1
140 PRINT "INPUT MEAN JOB TIME (HRS)";
150 INPUT L2
160 PRINT "INPUT MIN. SETTING UP TIME (HRS)";
170 INPUT S
180 PRINT "INPUT TOTAL NO. OF JOBS";
190 INPUT N
200 LET P=RND(-1)
210 LET A(0)=0
220 LET L(0)=0
230 LET W=0
240 FOR I=1 TO N
250 LET L0=L1
260              GOSUB 900
270 LET A(I)=A(I-1)+T
280 LET L0=L2
290              GOSUB 900
300 LET D=L(I-1)-A(I)
310 IF D>0 THEN 340
320 LET L(I)=A(I)+T+S
330 GO TO 370
340 IF I<11 THEN 360
350 LET W=W+D
360 LET L(I)=L(I-1)+T+S
370 NEXT I
380 LET W=W/(N-10)
390 PRINT
400 PRINT "NO. OF JOBS CONSIDERED = ";N-10
410 PRINT "MEAN WAITING TIME = ";W;"HRS"
420 PRINT
430 GO TO 999
900 LET P=RND(0)
910 LET T=-L0*LOG(P)
920 RETURN
999 END
```

```
← RUN
            RUN PROCEEDING
INPUT MEAN ARRIVAL INTERVAL (HRS)← 1.25
INPUT MEAN JOB TIME (HRS)← 1
INPUT MIN. SETTING UP TIME (HRS)← 0.25
INPUT TOTAL NO. OF JOBS← 50

NO. OF JOBS CONSIDERED =  40
MEAN WAITING TIME = 1.35056 HRS


            FINISHED
```

Figure 9.3 Program for queueing problem

Although this book has deliberately chosen to introduce BASIC statements by solving non-trivial and therefore (hopefully) interesting problems, there is a possibility that the details of problems may hide the programming techniques that we are introducing. So make sure that the point of this queueing-problem example is understood by looking again at figure 9.3 and studying how the subroutine (lines 900 to 920) is called twice (at lines 260 and 290), and in particular how the parameters (in this case just L0) have to be set before the subroutine is entered.

EXERCISES

9.1 Rewrite the programs of exercises 8.1 and 8.2 so that the functions in question are defined in subroutines instead of in DEF FN statements.

9.2 Write a BASIC subroutine to convert spherical polar coordinates (r, θ, ϕ) to Cartesian coordinates (x, y, z) using the formulae

$$x = r \cos \theta \cos \phi$$
$$y = r \sin \theta \cos \phi$$
$$z = r \sin \phi$$

Then write a BASIC program to

(a) input the spherical polar coordinates of two points (r_1, θ_1, ϕ_1) and (r_2, θ_2, ϕ_2)
(b) convert them both to Cartesian coordinates (x_1, y_1, z_1) and (x_2, y_2, z_2), using the subroutine
(c) calculate and output the distance d between them, where

$$d = \sqrt{[(x_1 - x_2)^2 + (y_1 - y_2)^2 + (z_1 - z_2)^2]}$$

9.3 Write a BASIC subroutine to calculate the inner-product $d(x, y)$ of two vectors x and y. (If $x = (x_1, x_2, \ldots, x_n)$ and $y = (y_1, y_2, \ldots, y_n)$ then d is defined by

$$d(x, y) = \sum_{i=1}^{n} x_i y_i \ )$$

The length of a vector x can be defined as $\sqrt{d(x, x)}$. Now write a BASIC program, incorporating the subroutine, to

(i) input an n by n array A and an n-element vector B
(ii) calculate the vector C = A B where

$$c_j = \sum_{i=1}^{n} a_{ji} b_i, \quad j = 1(1)n$$

(iii) compare the lengths of the vectors B and C, and output either

"B LONGER THAN C" or "C LONGER THAN B".

The subroutine will need to be called in (ii) (where $x_i = a_{ji}$ and $y_i = b_i$), and in (iii) (to calculate the lengths of the two vectors).

9.4 Imagine you are writing a program to analyse a large amount of, say, meteorological data. For the analysis to be acceptable the data must be carefully checked before they are analysed. In commercial computing systems analysts have brought such data validation to the state of a fine art. Here is a simplified version.

Let the data lines be batched into groups of a manageable size, each batch beginning with a header line. Each data line contains: line number, date (in the form XXYYZZ, where XX = the day, YY = the month, ZZ = the last two digits of the year), hours of sunshine, inches of rain, maximum and minimum temperature. On the header line are the batch number, the number of lines in the batch, and five check sums, one each for the dates, hours of sunshine, inches of rain, maximum and minimum temperatures. These are the sums of the relevant values on all the lines of the batch. Here is an example of a batch

```
9200 DATA 2,3,481686,9.7,0.2,61,25
9201 DATA 1,150562,3.2,0.1,22,8
9202 DATA 2,160562,3.9,0.0,20,9
9203 DATA 3,170562,2.6,0.1,19,8
```

(Normally a batch would contain rather more than three lines.)
Write BASIC subroutines as follows

(i) to output batch and line numbers and the message 'data error'
(ii) to output a batch number and the message 'sum check failed'.

Then write a BASIC program to input data in the form described above and to make the following checks

(a) that the batch numbers are sequential and start at 1
(b) that the line numbers in each batch are sequential and start at 1
(c) that the data are in the ranges

$010160 \leq$ date ≤ 311269
$0 \leq$ hours ≤ 10
$0 \leq$ inches ≤ 2
$0 \leq$ max. temp. ≤ 35
$-10 \leq$ min. temp. ≤ 15

with minimum temperature less than maximum temperature
(d) that each check sum tallies correctly
(e) that there are the correct number of lines in each batch.

In each case a failed check should produce an output message; subroutine (i) is to be used for each check in case (c), and similarly subroutine (ii) for each case in (d).

10 BASIC - MATRIX OPERATIONS

10.1 INTRODUCTION

At the end of chapter 7 we indicated that some of the tedious manipulation of arrays can be avoided in BASIC because the language has a set of powerful matrix statements. In these statements the arrays are manipulated as mathematical objects in themselves, as opposed to being manipulated element by element (which was the concern of chapter 7). The operations that are possible in BASIC are those that are most common in the subject of matrix algebra; so this chapter assumes an elementary knowledge of that subject.

Nevertheless we shall first of all summarise the matrix algebra definitions of those operations that are possible in BASIC. After that we shall describe the simpler matrix statements - addition, subtraction, transposition and the constant matrices - plus the matrix input/output statements. Then we shall revert to our previous approach by describing the first case study of the chapter - an electrical network problem - and introducing the extra matrix statements required to solve it; the same applies to the second case study - a vibration problem. Like the queueing example in the second half of chapter 9, the vibration problem is fairly advanced; both are included in the book in the hope that they will stimulate interest in the computer solution of technical problems.

A final point to note before we start on details, is that some small computer systems do not allow matrix statements. Because these computers have a restricted amount of working memory their BASIC facilities have to be curtailed correspondingly, and the matrix statements are usually the first to be omitted.

10.2 MATRIX ALGEBRA - A BRIEF SUMMARY

A matrix is a rectangular array of numbers, which is said to be m by n if it has m rows and n columns. Two matrices can be added together if they have the same dimensions, and the sum is defined by adding the matrices element by element. If A, B and C are all m by n matrices and if, for example, a_{ij} is the element of A in its ith row and jth column, then

$$A = B + C$$

means

$$a_{ij} = b_{ij} + c_{ij}$$

$i = 1(1)m$, $j = 1(1)n$. Subtraction is defined in the same way.

Matrices can be multiplied by scalars, or by other matrices. Scalar multiplication is defined as follows

$$A = kB$$

means

$$a_{ij} = kb_{ij}$$

$i = 1(1)m$, $j = 1(1)n$, A and B each being m by n. Matrix multiplication is more complicated; in particular BC is only defined if B has the same number of columns as C has rows. If B is m by n and C is n by p then

$$A = BC$$

means

$$a_{ij} = \sum_{k=1}^{n} b_{ik}c_{kj}$$

$i = 1(1)m$, $j = 1(1)p$, and A will be m by p as a result. Note that not only is $CB \neq BC$ in general, but that CB may not even be defined.

If A is square (n by n say) and has a non-zero determinant, then the inverse of A (written A^{-1}) exists, is n by n, and satisfies

$$AA^{-1} = A^{-1}A = I$$

where I is the n by n identity matrix in which the diagonal elements all equal 1, and the off-diagonal elements all equal 0. An equivalent definition is such that if $AX = B$ has a unique solution vector X for any known vector B then A^{-1} exists and $X = A^{-1}B$.

Finally if A is an m by n matrix then its transpose A^T is n by m, and is defined by

$$(a^T)_{ij} = a_{ji}$$

$i = 1(1)n$, $j = 1(1)m$. In words: the rows of A^T are the columns of A (and the columns of A^T are the rows of A).

10.3 MATRIX STATEMENTS I

As we have said, the matrix statements allow arrays to be manipulated as arrays, rather than element by element. Nevertheless they are still arrays in the sense described in chapter 7, and elements can still be referred to individually by the name of the array followed by one or two subscripts. Arrays appearing in matrix statements must be dimensioned in a DIM statement, even if the maximum subscript is ten or less. Matrix statements ignore the existence of a zero subscript even in systems that allow such a subscript. All the matrix statements begin with the letters MAT.

Vectors used in matrix statements are taken to be column vectors.

If a row vector is required it must be set up as a one-row matrix. For example, if A is to be a row vector with twenty elements, it would be set up thus

    DIM A(1,20)

10.3.1 Input and output of matrices

The input of whole arrays can be achieved by the MAT READ and MAT INPUT statements. (MAT INPUT does not exist in some BASIC systems). Their formats are

    MAT READ arrayname1, arrayname2, etc.
    MAT INPUT arrayname1, arrayname2, etc.

The arrays are input row by row. So

    100 DIM R(4,4)
    110 MAT READ R
    120 DATA ...

is equivalent to

    100 DIM R(4,4)
    110 FOR I=1 TO 4
    111 FOR J=1 TO 4
    112 READ R(I,J)
    113 NEXT J
    114 NEXT I
    120 DATA ...

For the case study of section 10.4 we shall need to read a 4 by 4 matrix R and a four-element column vector E, so we shall need the statements

    100 DIM R(4,4),E(4)
    110 MAT READ R,E
    120 DATA ...

The items in the data list will be in the order: first row of R, second row of R, third row of R, fourth row of R, elements of E (in order from top and bottom, as usual for vectors). MAT INPUT, when available, calls for the array elements to be typed on the terminal a row at a time. (For a column vector this means an element at a time.)

The output of whole arrays is achieved by the MAT PRINT statement. The format is

MAT PRINT arrayname1 {comma or semicolon} arrayname2 {comma or semicolon} etc.

The arrays are printed quite separately: the first named array entirely, then the second named entirely, and so on. The form of printing is determined by the comma or semicolon *following* the array name, much as for the printing of ordinary variables. If the separator is a comma then each element is printed at the beginning of the next zone, if a semicolon then at the beginning of the next section. If the last item in the MAT PRINT statement is not followed by either a comma or a semicolon, then a comma is assumed. A new print line is started for each row. Figure 10.1 shows a program and resulting output at the beginning of which a matrix is input from a data list and then printed with both possible forms. It should be clear that using the semicolon form *may* result in a jumbled output, since the position of the first digit of a number is determined by the number of digits printed in the previous number.

If a row is too long for one print line it is continued on the next print line, so even with the comma form arrays with more than five columns will tend to look jumbled. For example

```
100 DIM A(2,6)
110 MAT READ A
120 DATA 1,2,3,4,5,6,7,8,9,10,11,12
200 MAT PRINT A,
```

will produce the following output

1	2	3	4	5
6				
7	8	9	10	11
12				

Line 200 above is equivalent to

NEW OR OLD?
← OLD MATPRINT
← LIST

MATPRINT   ON 16/03/76 AT 19.01.46

```
100 REM MATRIX PRINT DEMO.
110 DIM A(2,4),B(2,4),C(4,2),P(3,3),Q(3,3)
120 MAT READ A
130 DATA 1,2,3,4,5,6,7,8
140 PRINT "COMMA FORM",
150 MAT PRINT A
160 PRINT "SEMICOLON FORM",
170 MAT PRINT A;
180 MAT C=TRN(A)
190 PRINT "TRANSPOSE",
200 MAT PRINT C;
210 MAT B=CON
220 MAT A=A-B
230 MAT PRINT A;B;
240 MAT P=IDN
250 MAT Q=ZER
260 MAT P=P+P
270 MAT PRINT P;Q;
280 END
```

← RUN
                RUN PROCEEDING
COMMA FORM

```
1                    2                    3                    4
5                    6                    7                    8
```

SEMICOLON FORM

```
1   2   3   4
5   6   7   8
```

TRANSPOSE

```
1   5
2   6
3   7
4   8
```


```
0   1   2   3
4   5   6   7
```


```
1   1   1   1
1   1   1   1
```


```
2   0   0
0   2   0
0   0   2
```


```
0   0   0
0   0   0
0   0   0
```

                FINISHED

Figure 10.1 Program illustrating matrix statements

```
200 FOR I=1 TO 2
201 PRINT
202 FOR J=1 TO 6
203 PRINT A(I,J),
204 NEXT J
205 NEXT I
206 PRINT
```

(Note the implication of line 206 that, regardless of the use of commas and semicolons, after the output of each array by a MAT PRINT statement subsequent printing starts at the beginning of a new line.) To avoid any confusion when the number of columns exceeds five the following is a possible alternative to the use of MAT PRINT (for an M by N matrix).

```
200 FOR I=1 TO M
201 PRINT "ROW";I
202 FOR J=1 TO N
203 PRINT A(I,J),
204 NEXT J
205 NEXT I
206 PRINT
```

For the example above the output would be

```
ROW 1
 1              2              3              4              5
 6

ROW 2
 7              8              9              10             11
 12
```

10.3.2 Constant matrices

There are matrix statements for setting up the identity matrix of any dimension

    MAT arrayname=IDN

for setting a matrix to contain all zeros

    MAT arrayname=ZER

and for setting a matrix to contain all ones

    MAT arrayname=CON

10.3.3 Addition and subtraction

These operations are achieved in the obvious way

    MAT arrayname1=arrayname2±arrayname3

There are no restrictions on the array names, so all of the following examples are valid.

```
    MAT A=B+C
    MAT A=A-B
    MAT A=A+A
```

On the other hand

```
    MAT A=B+C+D
```

is not allowed. In fact matrix statements in general must contain only one operation. B + C + D would be obtained as follows

```
    MAT E=C+D
    MAT A=B+E
```

10.3.4 Transposition

To transpose a matrix the MAT ... TRN statement is used with the format

```
    MAT arrayname1=TRN(arrayname2)
```
The two arraynames must be different, for example

```
    MAT B=TRN(A)
```

is allowed but

```
    MAT A=TRN(A)
```

is not.

It should now be possible to follow the program in figure 10.1 and understand why the resulting output is as shown. The program is designed just to illustrate the matrix statements described above.

10.4 CASE STUDY - AN ELECTRICAL NETWORK PROBLEM

Figure 10.2 shows a typical electrical bridge network, in which one or more of the resistors might be a sensor of some kind, that is, one for which the resistance will vary slightly if it is, for example, physically stressed. The network might then be used as a strain guage, a change in resistance being sensed by a consequent change in the electrical balance of the network.

A preliminary requirement in the design of such networks can be the checking that power levels implied do not overload the resistors; so Kirchhoff's laws may be used to calculate the loop currents

$$(R_1 + R_5 + R_6)I_1 - R_6I_2 - R_5I_4 = E_1 - E_5 + E_6$$

$$(R_2 + R_6 + R_7)I_2 - R_7I_3 - R_6I_1 = E_2 - E_6 + E_7$$

$$(R_3 + R_7 + R_8)I_3 - R_8I_4 - R_7I_2 = E_3 - E_7 + E_8$$

$$(R_4 + R_8 + R_5)I_4 - R_5I_1 - R_8I_3 = E_4 - E_8 + E_5$$

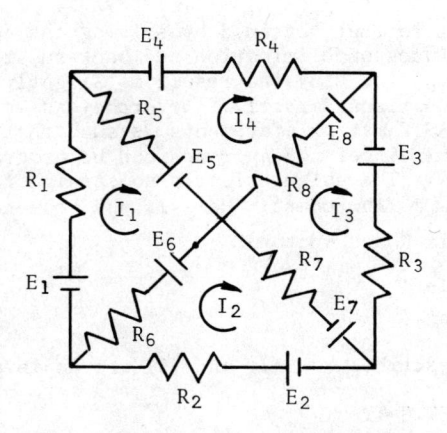

Figure 10.2 Network of case study 1

Assuming that the resistances and voltage sources are known quantities, this is a system of four simultaneous linear equations for the unknown loop current values. In matrix form the equations are

$$RI = E$$

where R is the 4 by 4 matrix

$$\begin{bmatrix} R_1 + R_5 + R_6 & -R_6 & 0 & -R_5 \\ -R_6 & R_2 + R_6 + R_7 & -R_7 & 0 \\ 0 & -R_7 & R_3 + R_7 + R_8 & -R_8 \\ -R_5 & 0 & -R_8 & R_4 + R_8 + R_5 \end{bmatrix}$$

I is the vector

$$\begin{bmatrix} I_1 \\ I_2 \\ I_3 \\ I_4 \end{bmatrix}$$

and E is the vector

$$\begin{bmatrix} E_1 - E_5 + E_6 \\ E_2 - E_6 + E_7 \\ E_3 - E_7 + E_8 \\ E_4 - E_8 + E_5 \end{bmatrix}$$

The solution (assuming it exists) is given by

$$I = R^{-1}E$$

which is equivalent to that obtained by solving the equations by the standard techniques of elimination and back-substitution. Inverting R and multiplying E by the result is slightly less efficient than solving the equations directly. Nevertheless we shall see that the power of the BASIC matrix statements is such that the simplicity with which the matrix inversion approach can be programmed outweighs all other arguments. The calculation is so straightforward that we shall not even draw a flow chart. Here is the sequence of operations

(1) Input the matrix R and vector E
(2) Invert R
(3) Compute I = $R^{-1}E$
(4) Print the vector I.

The next section describes how (2) and (3) are achieved in BASIC.

10.5 MATRIX STATEMENTS II

10.5.1 Matrix inversion

The inversion operation is achieved by the MAT ... INV statement with the format

    MAT arrayname1=INV(arrayname2)

Hence

    MAT A=INV(B)

leaves B^{-1} stored in the array A. If B^{-1} does not exist or if the calculation of it is inherently unstable (a real possibility) then a warning message is printed and execution will stop. The two array names must not be the same, so that MAT A=INV(A) is not allowed.

10.5.2 Matrix multiplication

To multiply two matrices together in BASIC requires a statement with the format

    MAT arrayname1=arrayname2*arrayname3

For example

    MAT A=B*C

The arrayname on the left of the equals sign must not appear on the right. So

    MAT A=A*B

is not valid but

    MAT A=B*B

is valid. As with addition only one operation is allowed in each statement, so A = BCD has to be programmed as follows

```
      MAT E=C*D
      MAT A=B*E
```

10.6 A PROGRAM FOR THE CASE STUDY

```
NEW OR OLD?
← OLD NETWORK
← LIST

NETWORK        ON 16/03/76 AT 18.41.20

100 REM BRIDGE NETWORK ANALYSIS
110 DIM R(4,4),S(4,4),I(4),E(4)
120 MAT READ R,E
130 MAT S=INV(R)
140 MAT I=S*E
150 PRINT "LOOP CURRENTS"
160 MAT PRINT I
170 DATA 3,0,0,-1
171 DATA 0,6,-1,0
172 DATA 0,-1,3,0
173 DATA -1,0,0,6
174 DATA 6,-1,3,-1
180 END

← RUN
              RUN PROCEEDING
LOOP CURRENTS


 2.05882
 0
 1
 .176471


              FINISHED
```
Figure 10.3 Program for the electrical network problem

Figure 10.3 shows a program to calculate the loop currents for the network of figure 10.1, with the resistances and voltages set at: $R_1 = R_3 = 2$, $R_2 = R_4 = 5$, $R_5 = R_7 = 1$, $R_6 = R_8 = 0$, $E_1 = 5$, $E_3 = 2$, $E_6 = E_8 = 1$, $E_2 = E_4 = E_5 = E_7 = 0$. (These values are not supposed to represent any particular application of the network.) The matrix R and vector E (see section 10.3) are correspondingly

$$R = \begin{bmatrix} 3 & 0 & 0 & -1 \\ 0 & 6 & -1 & 0 \\ 0 & -1 & 3 & 0 \\ -1 & 0 & 0 & 6 \end{bmatrix}$$

and

$$E = \begin{bmatrix} 6 \\ -1 \\ 3 \\ -1 \end{bmatrix}$$

The reader should be suitably impressed that such a small program solves the equations so easily. If not, then consider that the same program would solve a much larger set of equations by suitable changes to the DIM and DATA statements, and think how you would feel about having to write a program (without matrix statements) to solve n simultaneous linear equations, including checks for numerical instability.

10.7 A SECOND CASE STUDY - A VIBRATION PROBLEM

Figure 10.4 shows a simple model of a mechanical structure, in which the mass and stiffness of the structure have been represented by four rigid masses and some springs. The structure in this simple example can only vibrate in one direction but the principles of the analysis that we are about to make apply to more complicated examples such as the vibration of car bodies.

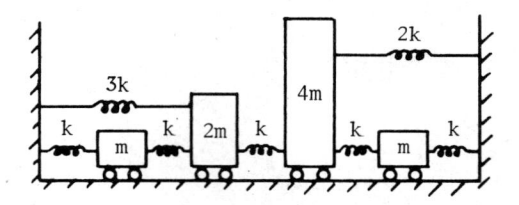

Figure 10.4 Model of structure of case study 2

We shall assume that the springs behave linearly, for all possible displacements, with stiffnesses (newtons/metre) as shown in figure 10.4. In that case Newton's second law of motion, applied to each mass in turn, gives the differential equations

$$m\ddot{x}_1 = k(x_2 - x_1) - kx_1$$
$$2m\ddot{x}_2 = k(x_1 - x_2) + k(x_3 - x_2) - 3kx_2$$
$$4m\ddot{x}_3 = k(x_2 - x_3) + k(x_4 - x_3) - 2kx_3$$
$$m\ddot{x}_4 = k(x_3 - x_4) - kx_4$$

where the x_is are the displacements of the four masses with respect to any fixed point, and $\ddot{x}_i = d^2x_i/dt^2$ where t is time. (These are not the complete differential equations but just the so-called homogeneous parts; they contain all the information about the vibrational properties of the system.)

A question that usually arises in relation to a structure like this is: can the system resonate? That is, can all the masses vibrate at the same frequency and in phase and, if so, what is the lowest resonant frequency and the associated mode (shape) of vibration?

If we assume that there are solutions to these equations in which all four masses vibrate at the same frequency and in phase, that is, that

$$x_i(t) = u_i \sin \omega t$$

where u_i is the amplitude of the motion of the ith mass and ω is the common frequency, then since $\ddot{x}_i = -\omega^2 u_i \sin \omega t$ the equations can be altered to

$$
\begin{aligned}
-\omega^2 m u_1 &= -2k u_1 + k u_2 \\
-2\omega^2 m u_2 &= k u_1 - 5k u_2 + k u_3 \\
-4\omega^2 m u_3 &= k u_2 - 4k u_3 + k u_4 \\
-\omega^2 m u_4 &= k u_3 - 2k u_4
\end{aligned}
$$

that is

$$
\begin{aligned}
\omega^2 m u_1/k &= 2.0 u_1 - 1.0 u_2 \\
\omega^2 m u_2/k &= -0.5 u_1 + 2.5 u_2 - 0.5 u_3 \\
\omega^2 m u_3/k &= -0.25 u_2 + 1.0 u_3 - 0.25 u_4 \\
\omega^2 m u_4/k &= -1.0 u_3 + 2.0 u_4
\end{aligned}
$$

Defining λ by $\lambda = \omega^2 m/k$ and A and U by

$$
A = \begin{bmatrix} 2 & -1 & 0 & 0 \\ -0.5 & 2.5 & -0.5 & 0 \\ 0 & -0.25 & 1 & -0.25 \\ 0 & 0 & -1 & 2 \end{bmatrix}
$$

$$
U = \begin{bmatrix} u_1 \\ u_2 \\ u_3 \\ u_4 \end{bmatrix}
$$

gives the equivalent matrix equation

$$\lambda U = AU$$

This is called an eigenvalue problem. Values of λ for which a solution exists are called eigenvalues, and corresponding vectors U are called eigenvectors.

There are pure mathematical methods for solving eigenvalue problems, but they are often not practicable. Since we only need to find the lowest resonant frequency ω, that is, the smallest eigenvalue λ, we can use an iterative numerical process called the Power Method. As with other methods used in this book we shall give only the briefest of descriptions of how it works. In the case of the Power Method see Ribbans[4] for a more complete presentation.

Normally the Power Method produces the largest eigenvalue and an associated eigenvector, but if we rewrite the last equation above as

$$A^{-1} U = (1/\lambda) U$$

we see that applying the Power Method to the matrix A^{-1} (assuming it exists) gives the largest value of $1/\lambda$, that is, the smallest eigenvalue λ of the original problem. This is called the Inverse Power Method and is the approach we shall use. Here is an outline of the method.

(1) Find a first approximation U to an eigenvector. If (as usual) there is little indication of what the eigenvector should be then try a vector whose elements are all one.
(2) Define a new vector V by $V = A^{-1}U$.
(3) Find M, the element of V of largest magnitude.
(4) Divide all the elements of V by M to give a new approximate eigenvector U, that is, $U = (1/M)V$ (U is said to be normalised).
(5) Go back to (2).

If the method works, we find that the sequence of values M and the sequence of vectors U converge, that is, become closer and closer to some fixed value $\bar{M}$ and fixed vector $\bar{U}$ respectively. In other words we get closer and closer to satisfying

$$\bar{U} = (1/\bar{M})V = (1/\bar{M})A^{-1}\bar{U}$$

that is

$$A^{-1}\bar{U} = \bar{M}\bar{U}$$

So the sequence of M values converges to an eigenvalue (and we can prove that it is the largest eigenvalue in the most usual case), and the sequence of U vectors converges to the associated eigenvector.

Figure 10.5 shows a flow chart for the Inverse Power Method. The only part that does not appear explicitly in the steps (1) to (5) above is the test for convergence of the sequence of M values. This is achieved by storing the old value of M in the variable E (which is set to zero before the loop starts) and then comparing the new value of M with E to decide whether to exit from the loop or not. Because we are considering the Inverse Power Method we have to compute an inverse matrix at the beginning and a reciprocal eigenvalue at the end.

10.8 MATRIX STATEMENTS III

The only new statement required to program the flow chart of figure 10.5 is that for scalar multiplication. Its format is

    MAT arrayname1=(expr)*arrayname2

where expr can be any arithmetic expression (including a single number or a single variable name). The brackets around expr are obligatory. For our case study we need

    MAT U=(1/M)*V

As another simple example consider

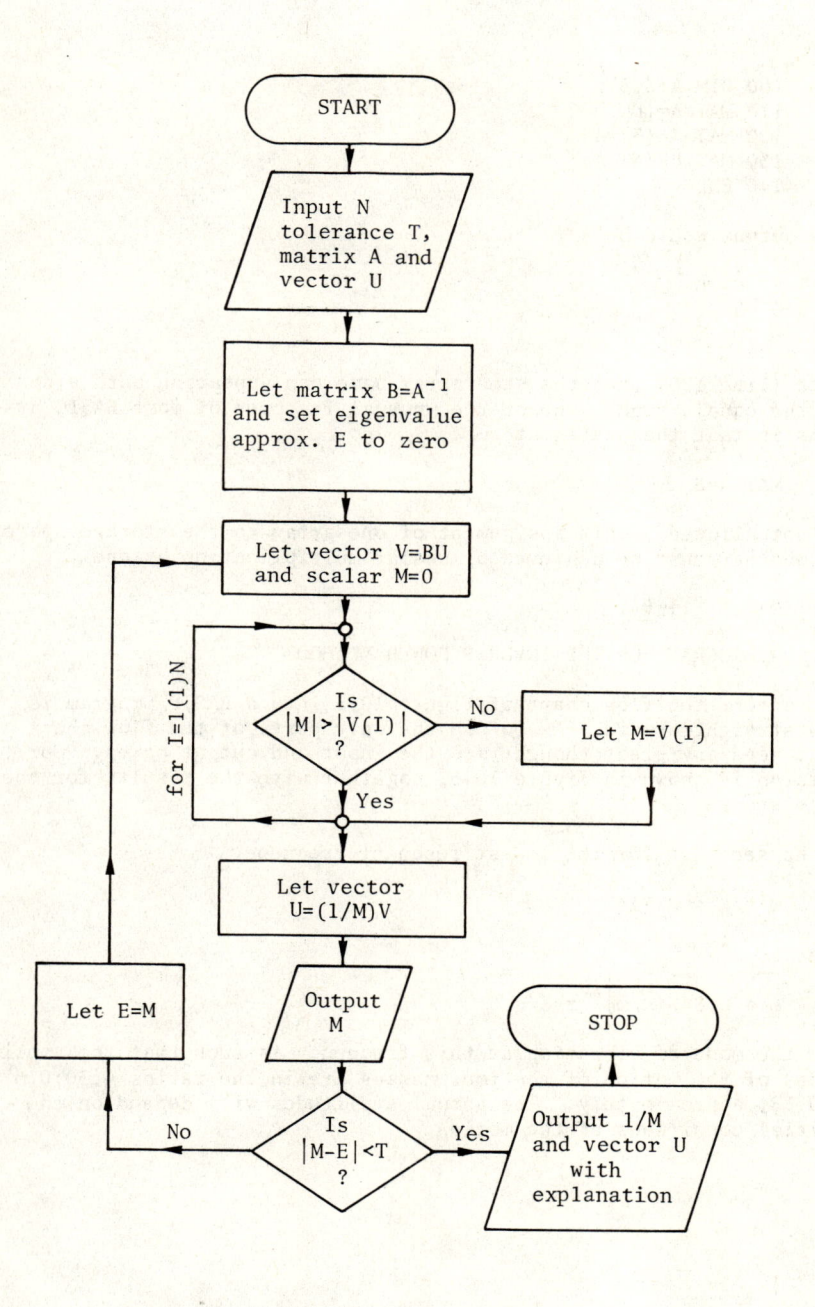

Fig 10.5 Flow chart for the inverse power method

```
100 DIM A(3,3)
110 MAT A=IDN
120 MAT A=(5)*A
130 MAT PRINT A;
140 END
```

The output would be

```
5 0 0
0 5 0
0 0 5
```

Note (line 120) that the same array name can appear on both sides of the equals sign. One of the unusual features of most BASIC systems is that the statement

MAT A=B

is not allowed. This assignment of one array to the storage space of another must be achieved by scalar multiplication by one

MAT A=(1)*B

10.9 A PROGRAM FOR THE INVERSE POWER METHOD

To convert the flow chart of figure 10.5 into a BASIC program is now straightforward. As before the only parts of the flow chart that need any great thought are the input and output boxes. Our version is shown in figure 10.6, together with the results for the case study.

We see that for the lowest resonant frequency

$\omega^2 m/k \simeq 0.714$

that is

$\omega \simeq 0.845 (k/m)^{\frac{1}{2}}$ rad/s

and the mode of vibration at this frequency is such that the amplitudes of the motion of the four masses are in the ratios 0.30:0.37:1:0.78, approximately. The actual amplitudes will depend on the initial conditions of the motion.

```
NEW OR OLD?
← OLD INVPWR
← LIST

INVPWR          ON 16/03/76 AT 18.50.47

100 REM LOWEST RESONANT FREQ. BY INVERSE POWER METHOD
110 DIM A(4,4),B(4,4),U(4),V(4)
120 PRINT "INPUT N, WHERE MATRIX IS NXN";
130 INPUT N
140 PRINT "INPUT MAX. ACCEPTABLE DIFF. BETWEEN"
150 PRINT "SUCCESSIVE ESTIMATES OF THE EIGENVALUE";
160 INPUT T
170 REM READ MATRIX A AND STARTING VECTOR U
180 MAT READ A,U
190 MAT B=INV(A)
200 LET E=0
210 PRINT
220 PRINT "SEQUENCE OF"
230 PRINT "APPROX. EIGENVALUES"
300 MAT V=B*U
310 LET M=0
320 FOR I=1 TO N
330 IF ABS(M)>ABS(V(I)) THEN 350
340 LET M=V(I)
350 NEXT I
400 MAT U=(1/M)*V
410 PRINT M
420 IF ABS(M-E)<T THEN 500
430 LET E=M
440 GO TO 300
500 PRINT
510 PRINT "EIGENVALUE OF ORIGINAL PROBLEM IS",1/M
520 PRINT
530 PRINT "ASSOCIATED NORMALISED EIGENVECTOR IS",
540 MAT PRINT U
600 DATA 2,-1,0,0
601 DATA -0.5,2.5,-0.5,0
602 DATA 0,-0.25,1,-0.25
603 DATA 0,0,-1,2
604 DATA 1,1,1,1
999 END
```

```
← RUN
            RUN PROCEEDING
INPUT N, WHERE MATRIX IS NXN← 4
INPUT MAX. ACCEPTABLE DIFF. BETWEEN
SUCCESSIVE ESTIMATES OF THE EIGENVALUE← 0.005

SEQUENCE OF
APPROX. EIGENVALUES
 1.54237
 1.44589
 1.41572
 1.40475
 1.4004

EIGENVALUE OF ORIGINAL PROBLEM IS            .714079

ASSOCIATED NORMALISED EIGENVECTOR IS

 .295157
 .366389
1
 .777295


            FINISHED
```

Figure 10.6 Program for the inverse power method

10.10 POSTSCRIPT - REDIMENSIONING

Some of the matrix statements allow the arrays involved to be redimensioned. This facility is of limited value because the number of elements in any array must never exceed the number of elements originally specified in a DIM statement. The statements that allow redimensioning are: MAT ... ZER, MAT ... CON, MAT ... IDN, MAT READ and MAT INPUT (when available).

The redimensioning is achieved by writing the new maximum dimensions after the array name in the same way as in a DIM statement. The new dimension can be any arithmetic expression - if the value is not an integer it is truncated to an integer. Here are some valid redimensioning statements.

```
100 DIM A(12,12),B(2,6)
110 MAT B=ZER(6,2)
120 MAT B=IDN(3,3)
130 MAT A=CON(1,100)
140 INPUT N
150 MAT READ A(N,2*N)
```

Note that B starts with 12 elements (2 by 6), and that subsequent redimensioning uses at most 12 elements (6 by 2 = 12 elements at line 110; 3 by 3 = 9 elements at line 120). Similarly A must never have more than 144 elements (so $2N^2 \leq 144$ at line 140).

The facility for redimensioning has two applications. It can save storage requirements by using one array to do more than one job in a program. In this case its dimensions in the DIM statement must be such that the number of elements is the largest that will be needed. Secondly, redimensioning allows a simple form of 'dynamic array bound'. For example, if a program is written involving an array A whose dimensions will vary according to the application, and if the total number of elements of A is unlikely to exceed 200 say, then

```
100 DIM A(1,200)
110 INPUT M,N
120 MAT A=ZER(M,N)
```

allows the required dimensions of A to be set by the input of the two numbers M and N. The disadvantage of this is that 200-M*N storage spaces remain unused. If a 10 by 5 array is required, for example, then 150 storage spaces are lying idle. Since statements are so easily changed in BASIC it seems more sensible, and not much more trouble, simply to type

```
100 DIM A(10,5)
```

before running the program.

EXERCISES

10.1 Write a BASIC program to input a square matrix A, and to test whether A is symmetric ($A=A^T$), anti-symmetric ($A=-A^T$) or neither. A suitable message should be printed giving the result of the test.

10.2 Write a BASIC program to illustrate the linear algebraic identities

$$(AB)^{-1} = B^{-1}A^{-1}$$
$$(AB)^T = B^T A^T$$

10.3 Suppose you are given n data points with coordinates (x_1, y_1), (x_2, y_2), ..., (x_n, y_n), and wish to fit a polynomial curve to the data, in the least-squares sense. That is, to find $a_1, a_2, ..., a_m$, a_{m+1} (m < n) such that

$$S = \sum_{i=1}^{n} [y_i - (a_1 + a_2 x_i + a_3 x_i^2 + ... + a_{m+1} x_i^m)]^2$$

is as small as possible. The solution to this problem is given by the equation

$$C^T C A = C^T Y$$

where A is the vector of unknown coefficients $a_1, ..., a_{m+1}$, Y is the vector of data $y_1, ..., y_n$ and C is the n by m + 1 matrix whose elements are given by

$$c_{ij} = x_i^{j-1}$$

$i = 1(1)n$, $j = 1(1)m + 1$. Write a BASIC program to input the data points, construct C and find and output the solution $A = (C^T C)^{-1} C^T Y$. Also calculate and output the vector of errors $Y - CA$, and S, which equals $(Y - CA)^T (Y - CA)$. [Note that $(Y - CA)^T$ is a row vector with n elements - see section 10.2 - and that to calculate S using a matrix statement requires it to be dimensioned, even though it has only one value, that is, DIM S(1).]

10.4 There are various iterative methods for solving a set of linear equations $AX = B$, where A is a given N by N matrix, B a given vector with N elements and X the unknown vector with N elements. They are all based on recurrence relations of the form

$$X_{i+1} = MX_i + C$$

where the 'iteration matrix' M depends on A, and the vector C depends on A and B. In the simplest case, known as the Gauss-Jacobi method, the elements of M are given by

$$m_{ij} = \begin{cases} -a_{ij}/a_{ii} & \text{if } i \neq j \\ 0 & \text{if } i = j \end{cases}$$

and those of C by

$$c_i = b_i/a_{ii}$$

In matrix terms if D is the N by N matrix with the same diagonal elements as A, and all other elements zero, then $M = I - D^{-1}A$ where I is the indentity matrix, and $C = D^{-1}B$.

Write a BASIC program to input A and B, construct D, calculate M and C using matrix statements, and perform ten iterations of the Gauss-Jacobi method. The iteration does not need the storage of all the X_i vectors; if X is the latest approximation then

```
MAT Y=M*X
MAT X=Y+C
```

produces the next approximation. Each approximation should be printed so that the process can be visually checked for convergence.

Convergence to the solution, if one exists, will usually occur if the matrix A is diagonally dominant, that is, has diagonal elements 'rather larger' than its off-diagonal elements. Here is such a system, resulting from an approximate method for solving the diffusion equation $\partial u/\partial t = \partial^2 u/\partial x^2$

$$\begin{aligned}
4u_1 - u_2 &= 0.4 \\
-u_1 + 4u_2 - u_3 &= 0.8 \\
-u_2 + 4u_3 - u_4 &= 1.2 \\
-u_3 + 4u_4 - u_5 &= 1.6 \\
-2u_4 + 4u_5 &= 1.6
\end{aligned}$$

REFERENCES AND FURTHER READING

REFERENCES

1. H. P. Westman (ed.), *Reference Data for Radio Engineers*, 5th ed. (Sams, Indianapolis, 1968) p. 5-33.

2. Peter A. Stark, *Introduction to Numerical Methods* (Collier-Macmillan, London, 1970).

3. F. S. Hillier and G. J. Lieberman, *Introduction to Operations Research* (Holden-Day, San Francisco, 1967).

4. J. Ribbans, *Basic Numerical Analysis, Book 2* (Intertext, London, 1970).

FURTHER READING

Brand, T. E., and Sherlock, A. J., *Matrices: Pure and Applied* (Edward Arnold, London, 1970).
Chatfield, C., *Statistics for Technology* (Chapman & Hall, London, 1970).
Digital Equipment Corporation, *BASIC PLUS Language Manual*.
Fenner, Roger T., *Computing for Engineers* (Macmillan, London and Basingstoke, 1974).
Hillier, F. S., and Lieberman, G. J., *Introduction to Operations Research* (Holden-Day, San Francisco, 1967).
Hollingdale, S. H., and Tootill, G. C., *Electronic Computers* (Penguin, Harmondsworth, 1970).
Hunt, R., and Shelley, J., *Computers and Common Sense* (Prentice-Hall, Englewood Cliffs, N.J., 1975).
International Computers Ltd, *BASIC* (London, 1972).
Kemeny, J. G., and Kurtz, T. E., *BASIC Programming* (Wiley, Chichester, 1971).
Laver, F. J. M., *Introducing Computers* (H.M.S.O., 1969).
Nolan, R.L., *Introduction to Computing through BASIC Language* (Holt, Rinehart & Winston, London, 1974).
Ribbans, J., *Basic Numerical Analysis, Book 1* (Intertext, London, 1969).
Ribbans, J., *Basic Numerical Analysis, Book 2* (Intertext, London, 1970).
Stark, Peter A., *Introduction to Numerical Methods* (Collier-Macmillan, London, 1970).
Wheatley, D. M., and Unwin, A., *Algorithm Writer's Guide* (Longman, Harlow, 1973).
Williams, P. W., *Numerical Computation* (Nelson, London, 1972).

SOLUTIONS TO SELECTED EXERCISES

Space does not allow us to give solutions to all the exercises in the book. Generally speaking, we have chosen some of the simpler ones, on the grounds that the reader will need most encouragement in the initial stages of developing his programming technique. For the same reasons the answers given are not as full as might be expected: REMark statements are not used at all, and the use of descriptive output is minimal, both of these being trimmings to the essential structure of the programs. It is important to realise that there are no unique answers to the questions. Two equally proficient BASIC programmers are quite likely to produce different programs for any given problem; the answers given here are just those of the author.

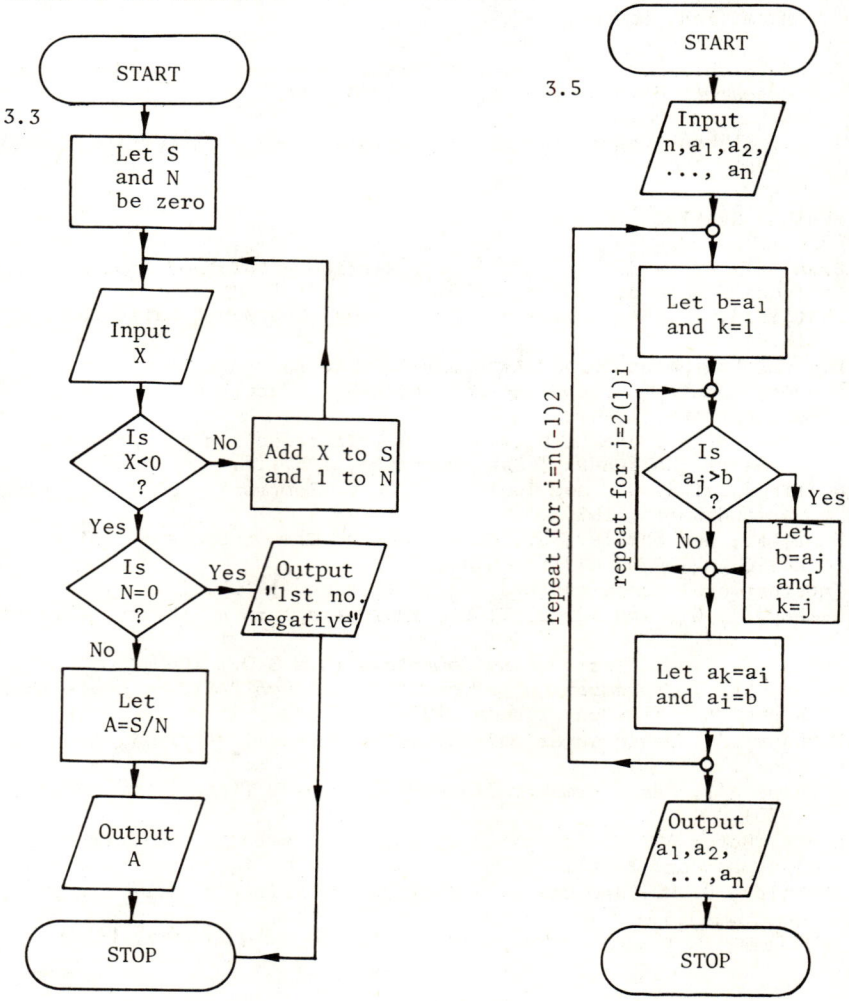

3.3

```
         START
           │
           ▼
      Let S and N
       be zero
           │
           ▼
        Input X
           │
           ▼
       Is X<0 ?  ──No──▶  Add X to S and 1 to N
          │Yes                    │
          ▼                       │
       Is N=0 ? ──Yes──▶ Output "1st no. negative"
          │No                     │
          ▼                       │
      Let A=S/N                   │
           │                      │
           ▼                      │
        Output A                  │
           │                      │
           ▼                      │
         STOP ◀────────────────────
```

3.5

```
         START
           │
           ▼
     Input n, a_1, a_2, ..., a_n
           │
           ▼
   ┌─ repeat for i=n(-1)2 ─┐
   │   Let b=a_1 and k=1    │
   │         │              │
   │   ┌─ repeat for j=2(1)i ─┐
   │   │    Is a_j>b ? ──Yes──▶ Let b=a_j and k=j
   │   │       │No                   │
   │   └───────┴─────────────────────┘
   │         │
   │   Let a_k=a_i and a_i=b
   └─────────┘
           │
           ▼
     Output a_1, a_2, ..., a_n
           │
           ▼
         STOP
```

```
4.2  100 PRINT "INPUT NO."
     110 INPUT X
     120 PRINT "NO. = ", X
     130 PRINT "SQUARE = ", X*X
     140 PRINT "SQ. ROOT = ", X**0.5
     150 END


4.4  100 PRINT "INPUT A1,A2,R,P"
     110 INPUT A1,A2,R,P
     120 LET B=2*R*P/(A1*A1-A2*A2)
     130 LET M=A1*A2*B**0.5
     140 PRINT "MASS FLOW = ", M
     150 END


5.2(3.3)
     100 LET S=0
     110 LET N=0
     120 INPUT X
     130 IF X<0 THEN 200
     140 LET S=S+X
     150 LET N=N+1
     160 GO TO 120
     200 IF N=0 THEN 300
     210 LET A=S/N
     220 PRINT "AVERAGE = "; A
     230 GO TO 999
     300 PRINT "1ST. NO. IS NEG."
     999 END


5.4  100 PRINT "X","Y","R",
             "DEG."
     110 INPUT X,Y
     120 IF X>1E9 THEN 999
     130 IF X=0 THEN 200
     140 LET T=ATN(Y/X)*
             57.29578
     150 LET T=T+90*(1-SGN(X))
             *SGN(Y)
     160 GO TO 300
     200 LET T=SGN(Y)*90
     300 LET R=SQR(X*X+Y*Y)
     310 PRINT X,Y,R,T
     320 GO TO 110
     999 END


6.1  100 IF A=0 THEN 210
     200 PRINT X
     300 IF ABS(X)<1E-6 THEN 370
     400 READ A,B,C
     500 DATA 3,5,9
     600 LET X=0
     601 LET Y=0


7.2(3.5)
     100 DIM A(20)
     110 READ N
     120 FOR I=1 TO N
     130 READ A(I)
     140 NEXT I
     200 FOR I=N TO 2 STEP -1
     210 LET B=A(1)
     220 LET K=1
     300 FOR J=2 TO I
     310 IF A(J)<=B THEN 340
     320 LET B=A(J)
     330 LET K=J
     340 NEXT J
     400 LET A(K)=A(I)
     410 LET A(I)=B
     420 NEXT I
     500 FOR I=1 TO N
     510 PRINT A(I),
     520 NEXT I
     530 PRINT
     900 DATA ...
     999 END


7.5  100 DIM I(4,4)
     110 FOR J=1 TO 4
     120 FOR K=1 TO 4
     130 LET I(J,K)=0
     140 NEXT K
     150 LET I(J,J)=1
     160 NEXT J
     200 FOR J=1 TO 4
     210 FOR K=1 TO 4
     220 PRINT I(J,K);
     230 NEXT K
     240 PRINT
     250 NEXT J
     999 END


7.6  100 DIM A(15,15)
     110 READ N,M
     120 FOR I=1 TO N
     130 FOR J=1 TO M
     140 READ A(I,J)
     150 NEXT J
     200 LET D=A(I,I)
     210 PRINT "ROW";I
     220 FOR J=1 TO M
     230 LET A(I,J)=A(I,J)/D
     240 PRINT A(I,J),
     250 NEXT J
     260 PRINT
     270 NEXT I
     900 DATA ...
     999 END
```

8.1 100 DEF FNA(X)=...
110 INPUT A,H,B
120 PRINT "X","F(X)"
130 FOR X=A TO B STEP H
140 PRINT X,FNA(X)
150 NEXT X
160 END

8.2 100 DEF FNA(X)=1+X+Y+X*Y
110 INPUT A,H,B
120 INPUT C,K,D
130 PRINT "X","Y","F(X,Y)"
140 FOR X=A TO B STEP H
150 FOR Y=C TO D STEP K
160 PRINT X,Y,FNA(X)
170 NEXT Y
180 NEXT X
190 END

Note The assignment of values of Y takes place in the FOR statement (line 150).

9.1(8.1)
110 INPUT A,H,B
120 PRINT "X","F(X)"
130 FOR X=A TO B STEP H
140 GOSUB 200
150 PRINT X,F
160 NEXT X
170 GO TO 999
200 F=...
210 RETURN
999 END

9.3 100 DIM X(9),Y(9),A(9,9),B(9),C(9)
110 GO TO 300
200 LET D=0
210 FOR I=1 TO N
220 LET D=X(I)*Y(I)+D
230 NEXT I
240 RETURN
300 READ N
310 FOR I=1 TO N
320 FOR J=1 TO N
330 READ A(I,J)
340 NEXT J
350 READ B(I)
360 NEXT J
400 FOR J=1 TO N
410 FOR I=1 TO N
420 LET X(I)=A(J,I)
430 LET Y(I)=B(I)
440 NEXT I
450 GOSUB 200
460 LET C(J)=D
470 NEXT J
500 FOR I=1 TO N
510 LET X(I)=B(I)
520 LET Y(I)=B(I)
530 NEXT I
540 GOSUB 200
550 B1=SQR(D)
600 FOR I=1 TO N
610 LET X(I)=C(I)
620 LET Y(I)=C(I)
630 NEXT I
640 GOSUB 200
650 LET C1=SQR(D)
700 IF B1>C1 THEN 730
710 PRINT "C LONGER THAN B"
720 GO TO 999
730 PRINT "B LONGER THAN C"
900 DATA ...
999 END

10.1 100 DIM A(20,20),B(20,20)
110 READ N
120 MAT READ A(N,N)
130 MAT B=ZER(N,N)
140 MAT B=TRN(A)
200 FOR I=1 TO N
210 FOR J=1 TO N
220 IF A(I,J)<>B(I,J) THEN 300
230 NEXT J
240 NEXT I
250 PRINT "MATRIX SYMM."
260 GO TO 999
300 FOR I=1 TO N
310 FOR J=1 TO N
320 IF A(I,J)<>-B(I,J) THEN 400
330 NEXT J
340 NEXT I
350 PRINT "MATRIX ANTI-SYMM."
360 GO TO 999
400 PRINT "MATRIX NEITHER SYMM. NOR ANTI-SYMM."
900 DATA ...
999 END

10.3 100 DIM S(1),X(30),Y(30),A(9)
101 DIM B(9),C(30,9),D(9,30)
102 DIM P(9,9)
110 READ N,M
120 MAT C=CON(N,M+1)
130 MAT READ X(N),Y(N)
140 FOR I=1 TO N
150 FOR J=2 TO M+1

```
160 LET C(I,J)=X(I)*C(I,J-1)
170 NEXT J
180 NEXT I
200 MAT D=ZER(M+1,N)
210 MAT B=ZER(M+1)
220 MAT P=ZER(M+1,M+1)
230 MAT A=ZER(M+1)
240 MAT D=TRN(C)
250 MAT B=D*Y
260 MAT P=D*C
270 MAT D=ZER(M+1,M+1)
280 MAT D=INV(P)
290 MAT A=D*B
300 PRINT "VECTOR OF COEFFS."
310 MATPRINT A
320 MAT X=C*A
330 MAT X=Y-X
340 PRINT "ERROR VECTOR"
350 MATPRINT X
360 MAT D=ZER(1,N)
370 MAT D=TRN(X)
380 MAT S=D*X
390 PRINT "SUM OF SQUARES=";S(1)
400 DATA ...
999 END
```